Developing Multi-professional Teamwork for Integrated Children's Services

Research, Policy, Practice

THIRD EDITION

Edited by Nick Frost and Mark Robinson

Mc
Graw
Hill
Education Open University Press

Open University Press
McGraw-Hill Education
8th Floor
338 Euston Road
London
NW1 3BH

email: enquiries@openup.co.uk
world wide web: www.openup.co.uk

and Two Penn Plaza, New York, NY 10121-2289, USA

First published 2006
Second edition published 2010
First published in this third edition 2016

A catalogue record of this book is available from the British Library

ISBN-13: 978-0-33-526396-7
ISBN-10: 0-33-526396-8
eISBN: 978-0-33-526397-4

Library of Congress Cataloging-in-Publication Data
CIP data applied for

Typeset by Aptara, Inc.

Fictitious names of companies, products, people, characters and/or data that may be
used herein (in case studies or in examples) are not intended to represent any real
individual, company, product or event.

Printed and bound by CPI Group (UK) Ltd, Croydon, CR0 4YY

Praise for this book

"Multi-professional teams are now recognised as an essential component of integrated care. Their key principles are well established, but we often struggle to apply these in practice due to challenging contexts and multiple priorities. Based on thorough research and relevant theory, this book successfully bridges the gap between academic insights and practitioner realities. In doing so, it should help to turn policy aspirations into real benefits for children, young people and their families. It is highly recommended to anyone who wishes to improve their own and their team's ability to work more effectively across professional boundaries."

Robin Miller, Co-Editor, Journal of Integrated Care and Senior Fellow, Health Services Management Centre, University of Birmingham, UK

"This is a very readable and well-constructed book which will be of benefit to any student or practitioner in the child welfare field. In a world of reducing resources, cross professional partnerships are vital in order to offer the very best services to children and their families. This book is a valuable contribution to this work as it offers both theoretical analysis and practical suggestions from experienced practitioners who are experts in their field."

Andy Lloyd, Head of Children's Workforce Development, Leeds City Council, UK

Contents

The contributors

Angela Anning is emeritus professor of early childhood education at the University of Leeds. Her background includes practice, training and research in the field of early childhood education and multi-agency childhood services, particularly in urban contexts.

Michael Cotton has been a teacher in special education, an educational psychologist and a service manager in local authorities in the North of England for more than 35 years. Latterly he has been working locally, regionally and nationally on the development and implementation of the 2014 legislative reforms for children and young people with special educational needs and disabilities, as a local authority manager and as a freelance trainer and consultant.

David Cottrell is foundation chair in child and adolescent psychiatry at the University of Leeds. He is a past associate medical director for child & adolescent psychiatry in Leeds and remains an active clinician as well as a researcher.

Jo Green is a research psychologist and was formerly deputy director of the Mother and Infant Research Unit at the University of Leeds. She moved to the University of York in 2004 where she is now professor emeritus.

Paul Hill has worked in children's services for more than 30 years, 27 of them in the same local authority. He has been a local safeguarding children board manager since 2006.

Julie Jenkins is a professionally qualified social worker and has led and managed early intervention, social care, youth offending, troubled families and youth services in several local authorities. She completed a masters degree in public policy and management, focusing her dissertation on leadership of integrated children's services. She takes an active part in the development of children's services staff in the Yorkshire and Humber region, utilizing the 'Children Social Work Matters' website to communicate with teams.

Melanie John-Ross is a senior manager in local government who has 25 years of experience as a social work practitioner and manager in children's social work services. She is passionate about supporting and developing social work practice to improve the life experiences and outcomes of children and young people. In

2012–13 she undertook research using a case study approach to understand the experience, impact and learning from the implementation of a multi-disciplinary children's assessment team in a large English metropolitan district with high levels of deprivation.

Sue Richardson gained her PhD from Plymouth University for a study of multi-agency information-sharing in children's centres. She is now lecturer in organizational behaviour at the University of Bradford.

Part 1

Researching and understanding multi-professional teams – working with children and young people

Part 1 sets the scene for the book. It outlines the policy and workplace context for the primary study on which the book is based, describes the research methods used in the core research project and analyses the structure and management of multi-professional teams.

1

Working in a multi-professional world

Angela Anning and Nick Frost

Policy background – New Labour 1997–2010

The first edition of this book was published in 2006 when the New Labour agenda for the reform of public sector services was in full swing. However, there were always conflicting messages. On the one hand, the rhetoric of New Labour was to devolve decision-making about service delivery to local communities and to give greater choice to users. On the other hand, there was a proliferation of central government initiatives to impose systems of accountability on those delivering services, such as evidence of value for money and performance management against set targets and national indicators.

Underpinning the Blair government imperative to 'modernize' (DETR 1999) was suspicion of the power held by local government 'professionals' (and indeed by local politicians). The workforces in schools, hospitals, social care and crime control were criticized relentlessly in the tone and substance of government publications. The implications were that professionals were primarily concerned with defending their vested interests and were bedevilled by over-staffing, bureaucracy, duplication and time-wasting.

The barrage of negativity from central government was fuelled by intense media coverage of 'failures' in UK systems charged with educating, treating, supporting, safeguarding and controlling children and their families. Notable examples were high profile cases of child abuse where children had 'fallen through the net' of protection, accusations of low standards of literacy and numeracy in primary schools and reports of the misuse of children's body parts without parental consent for medical research.

New Labour ideology acknowledged the interconnectedness of social and economic problems. In many ways, the 'Third Way' initiatives involving public sector service reforms reflected those begun during the previous Conservative Party decade, based on the ideologies of 'market forces', 'value for money' and 'freedom of choice for consumers'. But the difference was that Thatcherism in the 1980s and 1990s was premised on non-intervention in family life, whereas Blairism was more paternalistic. For both parties, public sector reforms were as much political as practical. But had the Conservatives not achieved their political imperative of disempowering unions in the UK, it is unlikely that the public sector would have tolerated the radical and rapid changes in working contracts and conditions imposed subsequently by a Labour government. So the histories of successive government policies in the UK are intertwined.

Positive calls for interconnectedness and negative critiques of old-style public service monoliths generated a new mantra for policy-makers – 'joined-up working'. The idea was that 'joined-up working' or 'thinking' acknowledged the interrelatedness of children and family needs in the fields of health, education, social services, law enforcement, housing, employment and family support. The aim was to reshape services. The belief was that joined-up working would make services more flexible, more responsive to local demographics and priorities, more efficient by reducing overlap of treatments, diagnoses and records, and ultimately more effective.

In particular, joined-up working was a central tenet of New Labour policy for reducing poverty and social exclusion. For example, the original construct of Sure Start, the New Labour flagship anti-poverty initiative launched in 1998, costed at £1.4 billion over six years and a prime example of a social intervention initiative, was that all families with children aged under 4 in the 500 most deprived areas of England would be offered flexible, accessible, affordable 'joined-up services' (Glass 1999). The 'treatments' were to be negotiated with local communties and were to support them in escaping the poverty trap. Early reports from the National Evaluation of Sure Start (NESS) of the impact of the early intervention on child and family outcomes were disappointing (Belsky et al. 2007) and created sufficient panic in the government for it to unravel Sure Start Local Programmes (SSLPs) and rebrand (many of) them as Sure Start Children's Centres (see www.ness.bbk.ac.uk for reports by the NESS team). However, there was good news too. Some SSLPs were achieving better outcomes than others (Anning and Ball 2008) and the characteristics of these programmes were fed into the guidance notes for the Children's Centres. As researchers would have predicted, by 2008, during which time children and their families in SSLP communities had been exposed to SSLP services for a substantial period, a variety of beneficial effects had been detected for children and their families when the children were 3 (NESS 2008). By this time the policy machinery had rolled on, leaving these encouraging findings buried in a plethora of new anti-poverty initiatives.

Throughout a decade or more of Labour government (1997–2010) a raft of cross-departmental government papers were published to promote the implementation of integrated services. They culminated in the Green Paper, *Every Child Matters* (DfES 2003), *Every Child Matters: Change for Children* (DfES 2004) and the subsequent Children Act 2004, which built on the seminal Children Act of 1989.

There were five outcomes for children and young people that embodied the principles central to the Children Act 2004: being healthy, staying safe, enjoying and achieving, making a positive contribution and economic well-being. These five outcomes became a mantra for the delivery and inspection of services for children in England.

The Children Act 2004 required every local authority to appoint a senior officer responsible for coordinating children's services (see Chapter 9 of this book). Local authorities were charged with developing Children and Young People's Plans by 2006 and establishing Children's Trust arrangements for allocating funding streams to children's services by 2008. In the government documentation, 'childhood' encompassed all children from birth to the end of secondary school and the focus was on developing the integrated delivery of services. All agencies, including health, were to share information and assessment protocols and frameworks. They were to plan jointly funding streams and intervention strategies.

Children's Centres (initially in areas defined as deprived but eventually in every neighbourhood, giving a total of 3,500 nationwide by 2010) were established as the base for the delivery of integrated services for children under school age and their families. Extended schools, both mainstream and special, were to serve as the hub of services for school-aged pupils and their parents. They were expected to provide: high-quality wraparound childcare before and after school, available 8 a.m.–6 p.m. all year; out of school activities such as drama, dance, sport, homework clubs, learning a foreign language, hobbies, business and enterprise opportunities, plus visits to galleries and museums; parenting support; referral to specialist support such as speech therapy or behaviour support; and family learning opportunities. Many schools are struggling to come to terms with this ambitious agenda. In 2008, *The 21st Century School: A Transformation in Education* (DCSF 2008c) reinforced the Every Child Matters agenda. Key principles were: powerful partnerships with parents, a resource for the whole community, promoting excellence in teaching and learning and 'narrowing the gap' between high and low attainments, and being at the centre of early intervention.

Meanwhile, agency-specific papers and guidance notes were also coming thick and fast, but embedded in all of them was the principle of agencies working together. For example, in health, a National CAMHS review was instigated with the twin objectives of investigating what progress had been made since the publication of *The National Framework for Children, Young People and Maternity Services* (DfES/DoH 2004a) and *Every Child Matters* (DfES 2003), and suggesting practical solutions for delivering better outcomes and monitoring those solutions. The resulting report, *Children and Young People in Mind: The Final Report of the National CAMHS Review* (DCSF/DoH 2008), noted a 'sea change' in the development and delivery of services and significant progress, but also made a number of far-reaching recommendations for further work. Specific recommendations addressed promoting understanding and involvement of young people and their parents and carers; better organization and integration of services to provide lead professionals as a main point of contact; clear signposting to specialist help; individualized and integrated care; effective transition to adult services and the establishment of a National Advisory Council; strengthening of the multi-agency national support programme; and inclusion of emotional and mental health issues in core children's workforce training. Throughout the report there are references to the importance of emotional health being everybody's business and the need for agencies to work together.

Building on Lord Darzi's NHS Next Stage Review, *High Quality Care for All* (DoH 2008b) and *The Children's Plan* (DCSF 2007a), the Department of Health and the Department of Children, Schools and Families published a child health strategy to improve health outcomes for all children. It is clear that the 'working together' agenda is still at the forefront of government thinking with explicit references throughout to partnership working between health, local councils and the voluntary sector. As well as specific policy recommendations for different groups (pregnancy and early years, school-aged children, young people and children with acute or additional needs), the strategy makes recommendations about 'system-level transformation' concerning the strengthening of Children's Trust arrangements and cooperation and collaboration between agencies.

The Child Health Promotion Programme (CHPP) (DoH/DCSF 2008), also produced by the Department of Children, Schools and Families and the Department of Health, which focuses on pregnancy and the first five years of life, and the *Child Health Strategy* (DoH 2008a) feed directly into *The Children's Plan* (DCSF 2007a).

Joint working was seen as a priority, for example: 'It is important that PCTs make use of children's trust arrangements to work closely with local authorities to jointly plan and commission services to deliver the CHPP locally' (2007a: 7). The *Plan* goes on to outline a vision of 'integrated services' (2007a: 10) with health visitors leading multi-professional teams built across general practice and Sure Start Children's Centres.

In *Reaching Out: An Action Plan on Social Exclusion* (Cabinet Office 2006), the government announced it would test the Family Nurse Partnership (FNP) model of intensive home visiting for vulnerable first-time young mothers. A total of £30 million was allocated to support this over the spending review period from 2008/9 to 2010/11 and a randomized controlled trial commenced in 2009. Although one of the FNP's goals is to link families into Sure Start Children's Centres, the FNP is an exception to the trend of encouraging multi-agency working. Rather it is aiming to produce highly trained family nurses, all of whom have a midwifery/nursing background, who have sufficient breadth and depth that they can deal with many issues without needing to refer on, thus reducing the number of people working with one family.

The Childcare Act in 2006 built on earlier commitments to expand childcare. Key drivers of the Act were to improve the well-being of young children and to reduce child poverty and inequalities. Part-time free childcare/early education was offered to all 3- and 4-year-old children, and in 2008 the offer was extended in pilot projects to some 2-year-olds defined as 'vulnerable' and deemed as 'at risk' of low attainments at school entry.

In the field of child protection, the Children Act 1989 had already placed interagency work at the heart of the remit for social services. But it was in particular the Laming Report (Laming 2003) on the death of Victoria Climbié, a young girl whom 12 potential child protection interventions from different agencies had allegedly failed, that prompted the government to formalize procedures for moving towards the integration of children's services, with the aim of safeguarding children more effectively (Frost and Parton 2009). These arrangements were set out in the Children Act 2004 and its accompanying guidance. In November 2008, events surrounding the death of Baby Peter (initially known simply as 'Baby P') hit the headlines and had major ramifications for children's services. Lord Laming reported on the state of the safeguarding system following the death of Baby Peter in March 2009 (Laming 2009). This tragic child death led to reforms to the system of inspection, changes to the training of the social work and related professions and a government push towards further integration of children's services.

Yet despite all these well-intentioned policies, a UNICEF report (2007) on child well-being in the 21 richest countries in the world reported the UK as scoring the worst rates on five of the six dimensions of child wellbeing, including child poverty, poorest health outcomes for young people (including early sex and high levels of teenage pregnancies and early 'risky behaviours' such as substance abuse) and lowest scores on children's assessments of their self-esteem. Perhaps in shocked reaction to these shameful findings, an ambitious *Children's Plan* was published in late 2007 outlining 2020 goals for world-class ambitions for all children, better support for parents and a new era for children's play and positive activities for young people.

New Labour lost the 2010 election to a coalition of Conservatives and Liberal Democrats. What followed was a shift from a focus on state expenditure and investment to generate a new form of childhood as envisaged in the 'Children's Plan' to an approach aimed at reducing state expenditure and a programme that lacked the big central drive and vision of New Labour that we have outlined thus far.

Multi-professional work under the coalition government – 2010–15

In this chapter thus far we have seen how the New Labour project (1997–2010) made a major contribution to leading and developing multi-professional practice in England. This era came to a close with the election of May 2010, when a coalition of Conservative and Liberal Democrats came to power and remained so until

May 2015. It is argued here that this event marks a significant shift in the history of multi-professional working in England.

As far as one can tell the demise of the Every Child Matters programme was never formally announced: perhaps this is because no politician could possibly make a speech suggesting that 'every child no longer matters'! Certainly the phrase was no longer heard in Whitehall and the dedicated website was 'archived'. Key moments occurred: the (joined-up) Department for Children, Schools and Families was given the decidedly un-joined-up name of the Department for Education in May 2010; the leading organizational embodiment of joined-up working – the Children's Workforce Development Council – was abolished; the database to underpin multi-professional work, Contact Point, was also done away with. These policy announcements came rapidly following the formation of the coalition and perhaps unintentionally undermined the strong drive towards multi-professional working of the previous decade.

Analysis of coalition child welfare policy is difficult and complex: while New Labour had a clearly identifiable policy direction which was explicitly stated, no such clear policy emerged from the coalition. There are a number of reasons for this:

- tensions within the coalition between Conservatives and Liberal Democrats made a clear policy direction more difficult to devise;

- the rhetorical (rather than real) coalition commitment to 'localism' was a deliberate shift away from 'Big State' policy leadership, New Labour style;

- the related shift away from guidance and targets (again more rhetorical than real) makes policy direction more difficult to analyse;

- the underpinning theme of 'austerity' and reductions in public expenditure which had a profound impact on the nature and extent of public service delivery.

Thus while the Every Child Matters approach was clear, explicitly written-up and subject to a coherent implementation, we cannot perceive any such coalition policy: rather there was a collection of policy statements, legislation, resource announcements and responses to specific situations that provide a policy context rather than a clear policy direction. It is argued here that this context made multi-professional working more difficult and complex than it was under New Labour. What have been the key elements of this policy direction?

- The fragmenting of services has made multi-professional working more difficult. This applies mainly to health and education services: both fragmented profoundly under the coalition. This fragmentation has taken place in the name of choice. Thus in education we now have fee-paying schools, free schools, academies and local authority administered schools. The role of the local authority has as a result been severely undermined. In health we have NHS England, Public Health England, Clinical Commissioning Groups and a variety of trusts. In contrast with education the strategic role of the local authority has been strengthened through the creation of Health and Well-being Boards and local authorities being given responsibility for community nursing commissioning. It is argued here that the main intention of these polices has been to increase choice, through marketization and competition, but an unintended consequence has been to make multi-professional working more challenging.

• The streamlining of central government guidance and regulation has undermined the regulatory framework for multi-professional working. One prominent feature of the New Labour era was the production of copious sets of rules and regulations. In child protection this was epitomized by the publication *Working Together to Safeguard Children* (WTSC) (DCSF 2010). Parton has undertaken fascinating research exploring the decrease in the numbers of pages of WTSC from 399 in the 2010 version to 95 in the 2013 edition (Parton 2014: 129). The decrease in the size of WTSC under the coalition is significant, symbolizing the decline of central government guidance (with some notable exceptions) in relation to multi-disciplinary working. This applies also to Children's Trusts which were mandatory under New Labour but were no longer so under the coalition, again potentially undermining multi-disciplinary work with children and young people.

In summary we argue that policy announcements, abolition of key initiatives, fragmentation of services and deregulation have all worked against multi-disciplinary professional practice.

Multi-professional working under the Conservative government – 2015 onwards

At the time of writing (2015) the themes that emerged under the coalition government continued into the period of majority Conservative government. This was symbolized by the re-publication of WTSC (DfE 2015) immediately before the election. This version represented minor changes from the 2013 version – increasing the emphasis on child sexual exploitation, revising the criteria for serious case reviews and strengthening the role of the Local Safeguarding Children Boards (LSCBs).

Two of the trends identified above – austerity and the increasing fragmentation of health and education services – continued under the new government, representing challenges for effective multi-professional working.

The persistence of multi-disciplinary working

It will be argued in this section, despite the policy drift outlined above, that multi-disciplinary working has not only survived under the coalition but has actually strengthened. How can we explain this paradox? There are two key potential explanations that are explored below.

Firstly, and it can be argued that this is the most important point, child welfare professionals have committed themselves to multi-professional working. As we see in the chapters of this book that report on our research with front-line workers, they find such work challenging, fulfilling and enjoyable. Child welfare professionals have embraced multi-professional work in terms of an ideology and as a practice that is now embedded in structures – LSCBs, Children's Trusts, MASHs (multi-agency safeguarding hubs) and so forth. Secondly, while this book focuses on multi-professional working in child welfare, the push for such working is embedded more widely in contemporary society. The language of 'networking' will be found across the world and across the private, public and voluntary sectors. It is a response to the complexity of the modern world and the challenge of 'wicked problems' – such as the persistence of crime and poverty (Dunleavy 2010; Frost 2014a, 2014b).

Thus it can be argued that we are living through a paradox: government policy is fragmenting services and making multi-professional working more challenging, while child welfare professionals are increasingly 'working together' and enhancing and developing multi-professional working. The way forward and sustainability of multi-professional work is returned to in the concluding chapter of this book.

Policy into practice: terminology

For those who struggle to design and deliver integrated services, there can be confusion both at conceptual and practical levels in the implementation of government reform of public services.

Epistemological confusions arose as the terms to describe different forms of 'joined-up thinking' proliferated under New Labour. In the 1990s, the talk was of 'partnerships' between agencies (see e.g. Jamieson and Owen 2000) and 20 years on the word came back into fashion (e.g. the notion of partnership with parents implicit in the Children's Plan). Drawing on a review of research and policy Frost (2005: 13) suggested a hierarchy of terms to characterize a continuum in partnership:

- *Level 1*: cooperation – services work together toward consistent goals and complementary services, while maintaining their independence.
- *Level 2*: collaboration – services plan together and address issues of overlap, duplication and gaps in service provision towards common outcomes.
- *Level 3*: coordination – services work together in a planned and systematic manner towards shared and agreed goals.
- *Level 4*: merger/integration – different services become one organization in order to enhance service delivery (see Dunleavy 2010 for a reinterpretation of this analysis).

The terms 'multi-agency' and 'multi-professional work' entered the discourse of policy and practice in children's services during the 1990s. Sometimes multi-agency teams were drawn together from distinct agencies for a set period of time and with an independent project or task focus, as, for example, in Sure Start local programme interventions and more recently in child sexual exploitation teams, as explored in Chapter 12. For Sure Start anti-poverty intervention programmes, workers such as health visitors, midwives, care workers, play therapists, librarians, teachers, psychologists, adult educators and counsellors were appointed. Some were seconded for part of their week from mainstream agencies. Others were appointed full-time for the contracted period of the Sure Start local programme. Alternatively, a multi-agency team operated under the umbrella of one main agency brought together to work as a team by systemic/structural changes of the host agency. Examples of such teams were child and adolescent mental health teams in health, youth offending teams in the youth justice field and child sexual exploitation teams. Other groups of professionals came together as inter-agency teams for a particular case – for example, a child protection conference; or disparate professionals from different disciplines were drawn together regularly as intra-agency teams to review policies and practices in a particular field of work (Watson et al. 2002). An example is a group of inter-disciplinary health and medical professionals working on a rolling programme of planning services across a local authority for children with cancer.

As the joined-up working agenda became more established, the key concept became 'integration', a term which began to feature in the Every Child Matters agenda and was championed by the Children's Workforce Development Council (CWDC). During the early years of the twenty-first century we saw the emergence of new language as we have witnessed the organizational growth of new multi-professional settings known as hubs, pods and MASH.

Whatever the terminology used to describe their working principles and practices, teams delivering multi-agency services consist of personnel from a range of professional backgrounds. For professionals, a particular knowledge base, set of values, training and standing in the community at large give them a particular professional identity. Yet Frost (2001) argued that even the term 'professional' is problematic and fluid from a position where categorizations of professionalism are seen to be intricately linked to the use of knowledge and power in a changing world of work. However, we have chosen to use the term 'multi-professionalism' throughout this book as the most fitting construct to describe the coming together of workers from the traditional services for children of health, education, social services, crime reduction and family support into new configurations for delivering variations of joined-up services. As we will discuss in Chapter 3, the epistemological configuration of multi-professional services on paper may seem to promise joined-up working, but it is the way the teams are organized and managed (from both within and outside the team) that dictates how effectively they are able to work together as multi-professional teams in practice.

Policy into practice: what works?

Governments across the world often require public services to be closely monitored and evaluated so that any changes in practice are 'evidence-based'. The principle is that major programmes are phased in to allow time for testing, evaluating and, if necessary, adjusting. These procedures have been longer established and more widespread in the USA (Greenberg and Shroder 1997). A UK government review panel (Government Chief Social Researcher's Office 2005) argued that two types of pilot – impact pilots focused on measuring or assessing early outcomes, and process pilots focused on exploring methods of delivery and their cost effectiveness – are often blurred so that they seek to achieve both aims. The panel argued that evaluations are bedevilled by the complexity of what they are expected to deliver in terms of quick evidence of 'what works' in the social sciences. In reality, evaluations frequently become redundant before they have been allowed to run their course, as policy innovations at 'pilot' stages are quickly entrenched in governments' forward planning and political profiles. Thus government claims of evidence-based reforms may be spurious (see Bilson 2005).

Findings of government-funded research into the effectiveness of reforms may be buried by delay or obfuscation. But one would hope at least that evaluations funded by taxpayers might serve to enlighten and inform the public about the complex and intractable problems of delivering effective services for a diverse, multi-layered population in the UK. As Young et al. (2002: 223) argue: 'Research can serve the public good just as effectively when it seeks to enlighten and inform in the interests of generating wider public debate. Not evidence-based policy, but a broader evidence-informed society is the appropriate aim.'

If we look across the evaluation reports of a range of programmes in the UK during the period of New Labour public sector reforms, we find common dilemmas reported in the processes of implementing integrated services. For example, early findings, concerning multi-professional teamwork related to Children's Funds, Sure Start local programmes (www.ness.bbk.ac.uk) and meeting the needs of disabled children (Wheatley 2006) all reported common dilemmas: reconciling different professional beliefs and practices; managing workers on different pay scales and with different conditions of work; combining funding streams from distinct agency budgets; and the lack of joint training and opportunities for professional development for both leaders and led within teams.

Two independent reviews of research in the field were commissioned (Atkinson et al. 2007 and Robinson et al. 2008). Evidence of the impact of reforms on service providers is growing. Benefits include opportunities for professional development and improved communication and information-sharing between agencies. Drawing on activity theory, Warmington et al. (2004) argue that rather than rehearse time-consuming arguments about models of multi-agency work and their effectiveness, a more radical model might be to conceptualize loose, flexible arrangements of professional networks to collaborate on specific cases/problems in particular contexts at points of need. They refer to this construct as 'co-configuration'. Benefits for service users are less well substantiated (Dartington Social Research Unit 2004), though it has been argued that integrated services improve accessibility, speed up referrals and reduce the stigma attached to services. At the end of the first decade of the twenty-first century the jury was still out on the effectiveness of integrated services (see Special issue, *Children and Society* 2009).

More recent findings have been more positive (see Frost 2014a, 2014b). In particular the five stages of the Local Authority Research Consortium (LARC) studies have been more positive about multi-agency working in the field of early intervention (see Easton et al. 2013).

Theoretical frameworks

This book and the MATCh study of multi-professional working which is outlined below draw on two theoretical frameworks: Wenger's 'communities of practice' and Engestrom's activity theory. We will explore aspects of these frameworks, as well as other theoretical underpinnings we found useful, throughout the book. However, below is a brief account of some key aspects of Wenger and Engestrom's theoretical models germane to our understanding of working in a multi-professional world.

In the field of sociocultural psychology, Wenger (1998) argues that new knowledge is created in 'communities of practice' by the complementary processes of participation and reification. 'Participation', according to Wenger, is the daily, situated interactions and shared experiences of members of the community working towards common goals. Reification is the explication of versions of knowledge into representations such as documentation or artefacts.

Wenger highlights the importance of professionals' constructions of their identities in shared practices and learning within multi-professional teams. Members of teams work together to develop a community of practice characterized by a shared history of learning and social relationships. The processes of developing a community of practice include mutual engagement (co-participation), a joint enterprise (shared accountability), and shared repertoire (common discourses and concepts). For Wenger, identity is 'a way of talking about how learning changes who we are and creates personal histories of becoming in the context of our communities' (1998: 5). 'Identity' is indeed one of four main organizing concepts in Wenger's model, underpinning workplace learning, alongside 'meaning', 'practice' and 'community'. Wenger views identity dynamically within communities of practice. Individual identity trajectories are negotiated (1998: 154) in activities in the world of work. However, Wenger's primary concern is the social influence of communities of practice on identity transformation. He writes: 'participation involves creating an identity of participation, identity is constituted through relations of participation' (1998: 56). Wenger does not make a distinction between self- and other-ascriptions of an individual's professional identity. Jenkins (2002) views these two dimensions as interrelated and intrinsically social. But Wenger's work can be used to make the point that experienced professionals in multi-agency teams will have undergone different historic processes of both self-determination and social determination of their professional identity.

We also draw on Engestrom's (1999) activity theory in the field of knowledge creation and exchange. An important premise in Engestrom's model is that conflict is inevitable as tasks are redefined, reassigned and redistributed within changing organizations and teams in the world of work. His premise is that such conflicts must be articulated and debated openly if progress is to be made towards creating new forms of knowledge and practice. Engestrom argues that change should be anchored *down* to actions that are 'real' within workplaces while being simultaneously connected *up* to a clear vision for the future. He describes 'expansive learning cycles' (Engestrom 2001) in the workplace as when communities/teams come together with different knowledge, expertise and histories to pursue a common goal. In order to effect change, they must work through processes of articulating differences, exploring alternatives, modelling solutions, examining an agreed model and implementing activities.

As we have pointed out, the project team brought different knowledge, expertise and histories to our common goal of research into multi-agency teamwork from the fields of health, medicine, psychology, education and social work. It was salutary for us to experience our own expansive learning cycles as we attempted to articulate and explore distinct approaches to conceptualizing practice, reconcile differences in research methodologies and reach agreement about the activities of communicating our new knowledge to audiences in oral and written versions. We will explore these tensions as we tell the story of the MATCh project in the early chapters of this book.

The MATCh project

The research which stimulated this book and is outlined in Chapters 2–8 was based at the University of Leeds, UK. An independent research council, the Economic and Social Research Council (ESRC) funded the project, so the research team were free from any constraints in publicizing the findings. The project took place over a two-year period in 2002–4. The aim of the research was to explore the daily realities of delivering public and voluntary sector services by multi-agency teamwork. We worked with five well-established multi-agency teams, exemplary of the type of team operating in health, the voluntary sector and social policy in the UK.

We were particularly interested in analysing the knowledge bases and practices that professionals brought to the teams from their previous work. We wanted to explore how professionals shared knowledge, how they designed together new ways of delivering services and how they developed through their working activities new forms of professional knowledge both as a team and as individuals. We wanted to understand more about how teams confronted and resolved conflicts in terms of the causes of problems and beliefs about appropriate treatments or solutions. Finally, we wanted to be able to provide exemplars of good practice to help other professionals working towards joined-up working. The research team was itself multi-professional and represented a range of disciplines. Between us we had extensive experience of the practicalities of working as teachers, social workers, doctors and psychologists. Our academic disciplines included education of young children, education of deaf children, social work, sociology, medicine and psychology. Thus in some ways we reflected the multi-disciplinary nature of the teams we researched. To these findings we have added new chapters on leadership, information-sharing, child sexual exploitation and children with special needs.

Conclusion

In this chapter we presented the context for policy debates that led to a governmental focus on multi-professional teams to work with children and their families. We have explored how the government approach to multi-professional work with children and young people has changed over a two-decade period. We outlined two theoretical frameworks – those provided by 'communities of practice' and activity theory – that helped to inform our approach to the issues explored in this book. We have reported the broad aims of and rationale for this book.

2

Researching multi-professional teams

Jo Green

Introduction

There are a number of challenges to researching multi-professional teams. For example: Who should be studied? What aspects of their work? What sort of data should be collected? How should it be collected? These are basic questions of the sort that all researchers must address when planning a research study. To a large extent, those decisions depend on the precise nature of the research question. If, for example, we want to know whether multi-professional teams deliver services that are better or worse than other service providers, we would be interested primarily in *outcomes*. We would therefore need to find some proxy measure of 'quality' of service (e.g. reoffending rates for youth offending teams) and we would need to look at outcomes for a relatively large number of people, comparing those who had received services in different ways. We would probably also want to focus on the experiences of service recipients, perhaps with interviews or focus groups. These could also be outcome-focused (e.g. we could ask people to assess their satisfaction with the services received), or they could be trying to understand process: what was it about the ways in which services were provided that made a difference?

The questions being posed by our study were more concerned with process than with outcomes. Our goals were to understand the experiences of individuals working within multi-professional teams and the ways in which the teams themselves developed and functioned. This meant that our focus had to be on the professionals themselves, rather than on service recipients.

One of the goals of our study was to help practitioners coming together to work in multi-professional ways for the first time. Our assumption was that there were useful lessons to be learnt from multi-professional teams who are established and apparently successful. The purpose of this study was therefore to try and understand how such teams make joined-up services a reality and to look at some of the implications of this. Specifically, the research objectives were to do the following:

1   Collect evidence about how multi-professional teams work towards their common purpose of providing effective services for users.

2   Analyse which knowledge bases and practices professionals from a range of services bring to their new communities of practice.

3   Assess which new ways of working are emerging from the activity systems of the multi-professional teams.

4   Explore the impact of new ways of working on the participating professionals.

5   Consider the theoretical implications of the findings for conceptualizing good practice in multi-professional delivery of services in multi-professional teams.

These objectives determined our choice of methodology. We needed to devise methods which would allow us to explore the complex interplay of: (1) structural systems; (2) participants' experiences of knowledge redistribution; and (3) professional affiliations and personal feelings; in relation to evidence of (4) new ways of working. In addition, our data collection strategy was devised with an awareness of the need to minimize intrusion on team members.

The remainder of this chapter will present an account of the methods used in our study, putting this in the context of the many choices that we as researchers needed to make. Primary considerations were always a focus on the questions that we were trying to answer and respect for research participants. The challenge was therefore to devise methods which would yield the necessary information without being overly intrusive and onerous to participants. These considerations permeated the entire research process, not just the gathering of data, since we were always aware that the need to respect participants' anonymity could create dilemmas for us in reporting our findings.

Data collection methods

Documentary data

The first stage of data collection was to gather existing documents: terms of reference; agendas; minutes; annual plans; guidelines for practice; regulations; and induction packs. The collection of documentary data was seen as important for a variety of reasons. First, what is documented, and how, represents primary data about how a team functions. Second, it was a way for us to start to become acquainted with each team and its activities in a non-intrusive way. Third, from both theoretical and practical interest in workplace activity and learning we wanted to try and understand the interplay between documented rules and records and team members' participation in activities, applying the conceptual framework developed by Wenger: 'Participation and reification transform their relation; they do not translate into each other ... participation and reification describe an interplay' (Wenger 1998: 68).

Observations of team meetings

Reading documents can tell us only so much about how a team functions. A team is made up of individuals and to understand how those individuals make up a team it is necessary to understand how they interact with each other. Team meetings offer the ideal opportunity to observe interactions between members and to gain insight into how decisions are reached and disagreements resolved. Team meetings are under-researched but they provide one of the few opportunities to see a team together as an ensemble. They are, furthermore, likely to be the major forum for interaction and decision-making. We thought it likely that these activities would be critical to a team's success. We therefore saw observation of team meetings as a key part of the data collection process.

One-to-one interviews

Documentation and observation of meetings would supply much of the basic information that we required. However, it was unlikely that these data sources would tell us very much about the team members as individuals: how they felt about their role and especially about issues to do with professional knowledge. One-to-one interviews were felt to be the most effective method for eliciting such information.

Critical incidents

The ways in which a team works are occasionally put to the test by specific 'critical incidents' or dilemmas. We were interested both in what sorts of incident caused problems for the team and in how team members worked together to resolve them. Given the relative rarity of these events, we could not guarantee that we would have the opportunity to observe them in team meetings. An alternative strategy was to ask team members to keep a 'critical incident' diary for a period of time. The diaries would give us information about the nature of dilemmas and how they were similar or different for different teams. They would, at best, only give us indirect information about how they were resolved. Our strategy to address this was to use the reported incidents as a basis for constructing fictionalized dilemmas for discussion with small focus groups from each team.

Choice of teams

Clearly the choice of teams for our study was important. Given the study objectives, we needed to recruit teams that we knew were well established with a comparatively stable workforce. We also had to be pragmatic. Despite our principle of minimizing the burden for participants, we were still going to be asking a lot of these individuals. We wanted to maximize the probability that the teams approached would agree to take part and that, having agreed, they would stay in the study. Putting ourselves in their shoes, we recognized that they would have to trust us and, in order to trust us, they would probably need to know at least one of us already. We therefore limited our list of potential teams to those with whom we had pre-existing links. Given the varied backgrounds of the research team (health, education and social work), this was not a major limitation. We then wanted to ensure that the teams we approached would represent a range of different vignettes, for example, different lead agencies and different client groups. This produced a list of five teams. This was felt to be a maximum number for the level of in-depth study that we were proposing. All five teams were approached before submission of the funding application and all five agreed to take part at that stage. Because there is an inevitable time-lag between writing a funding application and starting the research, we expected that the teams' circumstances would change and that at least one or two would drop out. In fact, one team did consider withdrawing, but in the end all five remained in the study. Details of the five teams are given in Chapter 3.

Phases of the research

Phase 1

The teams were first approached when the tender was being prepared. They were re-contacted once funding had been confirmed. When the research fellow started, he contacted the teams to introduce himself and to obtain documentation. He arranged to attend a team meeting with each team, this time with another member of the research team. The rationale for this was twofold: first, to give a second perspective and, second, so that members of the research team could meet the participants and vice versa. We did this only for the second team meeting because we felt that two researchers attending the first meeting might seem intimidating.

Observation of interaction in group meetings is challenging, both ethically and practically. We made every effort to be unobtrusive at meetings, sitting slightly outside the main group if this was possible. The project team members gave consent for tape-recording individual interviews but, due to concerns about confidentiality, not for having meetings recorded. Detailed field notes were made on the main topics, contours of discussion and decision-taking processes to record team members' participation in the workplace (daily situated interactions and shared experiences). To explore team interactions, the researchers drew seating plans (see Chapter 5, for an example) and diagrams showing turn-taking by different professionals during two episodes at each meeting. The researchers also collected meeting agendas, minutes and documents circulated as examples of reification (explications of professional knowledge in representations such as policy documents, team plans, minutes, rules and rituals).

The documents and field notes were analysed thematically. From the field notes, we noted key exchanges between participants and the diagrams showing interaction patterns gave us insights into patterns of dominance and dependence within key episodes of the teams' decision-making. Where such patterns were recurrent, this suggested they were significant. Our analysis of major content themes and of patterns of interaction was used to develop the interview topic schedule and inform the analysis of interviews at Phase 2. In particular, we explored the complex interplay of contextual/structural features of the teams (from document analysis) and the personal/professional dilemmas of the team members in generating new ways of working (from our observations and interviews).

Phase 2a: Interviews

The second phase of data collection had two stages. Phase 2a consisted of individual face-to-face interviews with selected members of the teams. It was necessary to be selective both because of the limitations of our own time and resources and to reduce the burden on the teams. Interviewees were selected to represent both the different disciplines and the different levels of seniority within each team. Views of other team members were later represented in the research through their key incident memos and through the focus groups. A total of 30 individuals were selected for interview (see Table 2.1) and access was negotiated through team managers.

All those selected agreed to be interviewed, and signed informed consent forms. Twenty-two interviews were conducted by the research fellow and eight by other members of the research team. In the latter case, the research team member would already have met the interviewee at a team meeting. All interviews were conducted at the interviewee's place of work and at a time of their choosing. Interviews were tape-recorded, with consent, and transcribed in full. Every effort was made to limit the interviews to one hour.

Interview schedule

The semi-structured interview schedule was designed specifically to explore issues related to three main areas:

- interviewees' experiences of sharing their professional knowledge and skills;
- the ways in which their knowledge is deployed in everyday activities in their team;
- their perceptions of the constraints and affordances of operationalizing 'joined-up thinking'.

Table 2.1 Interview participants

Team	Interview participants
Youth crime	A drugs worker, an education officer, a police officer, a probation officer, a nurse, a manager, a youth support worker, a social worker
Child mental health	A lead clinician, a manager, a senior child mental health practitioner, three child mental health practitioners
Special needs nursery	A team leader, a training and development officer, a special needs nursery nurse, a counsellor, a speech and language therapist
Neuro-rehabilitation	A teacher, a social worker, a doctor, a psychologist, an occupational therapist
Child development	A child psychologist, a health visitor, a special needs nursery nurse, a paediatrician, a physiotherapist, a social worker

Although these broad areas had been identified before the study started, by conducting the interviews after Phase 1 we were able to ask much more focused and grounded questions. There was no necessity to spend time on much of the background and contextual data-gathering that would have been necessary if the interviews had been our first contact. Furthermore, the interviewer was not a complete stranger and was known to have basic contextual knowledge about the team. All this meant that we were able to make the most effective use of the time spent one-to-one with the interviewees.

Analysis of interviews
Interview analysis focused on team members' perceptions of:

- their professional knowledge and skills;
- how knowledge is redistributed;
- the constraints and affordances of deploying professional knowledge in service delivery.

The tape-recordings were transcribed and analysed systematically, using dimensional analysis (Shatzman 1991). Nvivo software was used to support the data analysis.

Analysis involved a number of stages (Strauss and Corbin 1998). First was 'familiarization', repeated reading and rereading of the transcripts to get an overall feel for the content. From this it was possible to identify the themes that were common across the interviews. There were two kinds of themes: (1) those that were inevitably there as a result of the interview structure (e.g. 'sharing knowledge'); and (2) those that could be identified as being additional to those arising from the way in which respondents had answered the questions. All the themes were then integrated into a coding structure which allowed thematic coding of all the interviews. Once this had been done, it was possible to work with the coded data to develop ideas about how the themes linked together, and then to integrate them into thematic categories. This led on to interpreting the major themes: discerning patterns of meaning and explanatory concepts, and developing statements of relationships between influences, case incidents or patterns, and consequences.

'Generalization' was an ongoing aspect of the analysis. This meant ensuring that the themes and explanations that we were generating were not just one-off events and that they did provide an interpretative framework which was robust for the whole data set and beyond. This meant that the other data sources also had to be incorporated, and constant comparison of instances within and between phases was ongoing throughout. We paid particular attention to discrepancies and negative instances. Finally, we needed always to have our theoretical frameworks in mind and to reflect critically on how they did and did not fit with the empirical evidence.

Phase 2b: critical incident diaries

During Phase 2b all team members were asked to keep a critical incident diary. They were asked to record four or five examples of 'key episodes', occurring over three months. They were asked to describe key events, some positive and some challenging, involving issues of multi-agency team client-focused practice or knowledge-sharing, and not just incidents involving team meetings.

It was explained that the incidents would be used later in the project for the research team to develop invented vignette scenarios which teams would be invited to discuss in focus groups. Participants were assured that the diaries would be treated with absolute confidentiality.

Participants were given pro-formas for their diaries with the following headings:

- description of key event;
- date, place, who was involved, the history and build-up to the incident;
- your response;
- what you did immediately, and later;
- how the multi-agency team was involved;
- what team members and agencies were involved, what they did, immediately and later.

Eighty-one diaries were distributed and 30 different participants returned diaries. A total of 61 incidents were described. We identified the main themes in the diaries, considering only those incidents which conformed to our instructions to identify key episodes of multi-agency working. Many diaries did not describe specific incidents, while others did not describe incidents specifically relevant to multi-agency work. Eliminating those which did not conform, a total of 21 incidents were retained for analysis. From these 21, eliminating instances of repetition, 12 episodes were shortlisted by two members of the research team to draw on as a basis for developing vignettes. After reading and discussing these episodes, the entire research team then identified the following major themes for development into vignette scenarios:

- dilemmas of induction into a new team and threats to professional identity;
- dilemmas of changes of working practices – confidentiality/information-sharing and workspace issues;
- dilemmas of teams as communities of practice – membership defined by jargon – exclusion of incomers;
- dilemmas of liaison with professionals outside the team – inclusion;
- differing values of professionals and differing values of professionals and service users – implications for decision-making;
- dilemmas of devolving/mainstreaming of professional knowledge and skills.

Phase 3: focus groups

Six anonymized, fictional vignettes were constructed which drew directly on the themes identified in the diaries, and also indirectly on individual interviews. The six dilemmas concerned:

1   The tension between sharing expertise and acknowledging specialist expertise.

2   The reshaping of working practices, and negotiating a common way of working, with shared documentation.

3   Inclusion/exclusion of team members, for example, through the use of language within the team.

4   How you as a team would work to engage an external agency you feel is important to your core work.

5   How to resolve differences of values between team members and how to take account of the values of users.

6   Tensions arising from transferring skills to colleagues or users when people may feel short-changed by not accessing specialists.

Vignette 2.1

You are a psychologist working as part of a multi-agency team. One of the good things about your team is the way that everybody learns from everybody else so that you all broaden your skills. However, you are gradually becoming aware that there is a downside to this, which is that your colleagues no longer seem to recognize that you have specific expertise that they do not have. There has been discussion of a particular case that you consider requires specialist input from a psychologist, but your colleagues disagree and do not seem to feel that your view should have more weight than anybody else's. What do you do?

The dilemma here is the tension between sharing expertise and acknowledging specialist expertise.

Vignette 2.2

At your interview for joining the newly established multi-agency team as a specialist in paediatrics, much was made of the need to respect individual expertise/knowledge but at the same time aiming towards common working practices in the delivery of services.

When you questioned the manager about how this worked, the answers were vague. When you take up the post three months later, you discover that the team buildings have been refurbished. You are to share a communal working space. Storage of files for service users is to take place in a general office. You feel strongly that you need individual workspace and are used to having your own room and your own secure filing system and storage of user records. You are very anxious about issues of ethics and confidentiality. How do you deal with this?

The dilemma here is the reshaping of working practices, and negotiating a common way of working, with shared documentation.

Vignette 2.3

A new counsellor has joined your very well-functioning, friendly multi-agency team, which works with troubled children and their parents. At team meetings and in one-to-one settings it has been noted that the counsellor uses a lot of counselling jargon in their everyday interactions. The counsellor quotes theorists and techniques which are unfamiliar to the rest of the team. The team manager has approached the counsellor informally and pointed out that the use of jargon is excluding the other members of the team. The use of jargon has continued despite this intervention. You suspect that the counsellor feels that they have a low status within the team and that they are using jargon in an attempt to project professional competence. How would you approach this issue?

The dilemma here concerns inclusion/exclusion of team members, for example, through the use of language within the team.

Vignette 2.4

Your multi-agency team includes health and social services professionals working together. You have become aware of weak links with education (not represented in the team). To strengthen links, you have started to invite a 'liaison' professional to attend alternate weekly meetings and to share some joint client assessment work. The meetings discuss criteria for making agency resources available to your client group (children with complex special needs). Concerns have been raised that some children fall through the net, and that the agency puts up barriers.

After three meetings, a colleague alerts your team to a pattern at the meetings of team members blaming problems on the new person's agency, and saying that 'education' is not cooperative. Also, the visitor soon begins coming less often. Off-record, colleagues said that the visitor (an educational psychologist) does not share the same communication style as the team. How do you maintain your team's identity, while nurturing closer links with professionals in agencies whose cultural values seem very different?

The dilemma here is how you as a team would work to engage an external agency you feel is important to your core work.

Vignette 2.5

A front-line family worker is aware of the clash of values between members of the multi-agency team for which she works. In discussions of cases, decisions about what services should be made available to users are hotly debated by those from former social services, health and education backgrounds. But a further clash of values is apparent when she deals directly with service users. She is currently worried about a case of a lone parent father of a 3-year-old with complex special needs. There are concerns about discipline techniques and an alleged lack of 'nurturing' warmth. Some team members have previously felt that formal action should be taken with social services, and others have felt that this would destroy the chance of working collaboratively to resolve the problems. How do you think the family worker can best voice her concern in dealing with different values:

1   Of the team members?
2   Of the parent in responding to the rights and needs of the child within a family unit?

The dilemma here concerns how to resolve differences of values between team members and how to take account of the values of users.

Vignette 2.6

It is part of your multi-agency team's philosophy to pass your skills on to professionals in other agencies. This is partly a workload issue.

You have been involved in a project training mentors in schools to carry out work with children 'at risk' of exclusion. In particular, you have provided basic-level family work skills to mentors who work alongside individual children. A confrontation has developed in one participating school. A small group of parents complained to the headteacher that mentors are 'not sufficiently qualified or skilled' to advise families on parenting skills. Now the head is threatening to withdraw from the project, despite service level agreements having been agreed with the local authority.

How do you resolve such problems that may arise from passing your skills to other professionals?

The dilemma here concerns tensions arising from transferring skills to colleagues or users when people may feel short-changed by not accessing specialists.

Five focus groups were established, that is one per team. We requested named individuals to attend these groups, selected either because we felt that their presence was key or because they had not been included in the individual interviews. In practice, not all of those invited to attend were able to do so. In most cases the group discussion took place with a reduced number of participants; in a small number of cases substitutions were made by the team manager. Participants are shown in Table 2.2.

Focus groups lasted for one hour and were all conducted by the research fellow and one other member of the research team. With participants' permission, all were tape-recorded and transcribed. Each focus group was offered three

Table 2.2 Focus group participants

Team	Focus group participants
Youth crime	A drugs worker, an education officer, a team manager, a nurse, a probation officer, a youth support worker
Child mental health	A lead clinician, a manager, a senior child mental health practitioner, three child mental health practitioners
Special needs nursery	A training and development officer, a special needs nursery nurse, a portage home visitor, a special needs nursery coordinator, a speech and language therapist
Neuro-rehabilitation	A teacher, a physiotherapist, an occupational therapist
Child development	A paediatrician, a child psychologist, a physiotherapist, an occupational therapist, a special needs nursery nurse, a health visitor

vignettes to discuss. These were chosen such that each vignette was discussed by at least two groups. The matching of vignettes to teams was on the basis of likely relevance but avoiding giving a team a vignette which closely resembled one described in a diary by a member of that team. Nevertheless, a number of participants greeted a vignette with cries of recognition, suggesting that we had been successful in identifying vignettes that had resonance for these team members.

Validation event

After completion of all data collection and analysis we organized a feedback event to which all teams were invited to send five members.

The day had a number of purposes:

- to inform team members of our findings and interpretations;
- to seek their endorsement of our interpretations;
- to seek their endorsement of the ways in which we were using potentially identifying material;
- to encourage them to discuss emerging issues with members of the other teams.

The emergent findings were presented to the representatives from the teams and their views and opinions were noted. In the event, the team representatives largely validated the data we had gathered and it was not necessary to make any alterations or changes in emphasis.

Ethics and confidentiality

Ethical approval to conduct the research was obtained from the local research ethics committee. Information sheets were provided to all team members and written consent was obtained prior to interviews and focus groups. Participants were assured of confidentiality and a writing protocol for publications was adopted to ensure this. Thus, throughout this book we have endeavoured to protect participants' identities by using a generic approach – for example, 'one of the social workers', 'one of the professionals', wherever this is possible and not necessarily identifying their team if this would be likely to lead to their identification.

The issue of identifiability was one that we specifically raised with participants at the final validation event. Those present not only endorsed our interpretation of our findings, but also assured us that they were happy with the ways in which we were using potentially identifying material.

'Reflective practice'

'Reflective practice' is often urged on professionals of all disciplines. It had a particular meaning for us in carrying out this piece of research as we quickly realized that we were ourselves an example of that which we were studying. We not only had different professional training (as a teacher, social worker, doctor and psychologist) but also had very different professional trajectories and allegiances. Although, at the time of carrying out the research, we were all employed by the same university, we were in different departments which had different cultures and management styles. This awareness of ourselves as a multi-agency team allowed us to add another level of iteration to our research; we were ourselves another source of data, a 'reality check' for our emerging theories. Conversely, awareness of issues which were challenges for us, for example, different approaches to 'confidentiality', sensitized us to look for parallels in the teams we were studying.

Conclusion

This chapter has outlined the issues that we had to address in deciding how to gather data to answer our study questions. Our goals were to understand the experiences of individuals working within multi-professional teams and the ways in which the teams themselves developed and functioned. This meant that our focus was on the professionals themselves, rather than on service recipients. Our methods were chosen to give us a multi-faceted picture of participants' experiences and perspectives while minimizing the burden on them. We therefore used existing documentation and observation of team meetings as well as interviews, critical incident diaries and focus groups. So much data could have been overwhelming, but we were able to make efficient use of it, especially with the help of the data management software, and could feel confident that we had enough different data sources to substantiate our analysis. Analysis was an iterative process whereby emergent themes were constantly tested against the data themselves and the theoretical frameworks within which we were working. Finally, we validated our findings by presenting them both to team members and to other professionals for discussion and endorsement.

Two particular aspects of our methods were somewhat unusual. First, we gained a great many valuable insights by observing team meetings. This is not a widely used means of gathering data, but was one that we found very rich and which had the major advantage of not taking up any extra time from team members. It was ideal for a study like ours that was focused on teams, because team meetings were often the only time that the team came together. These observations were also a very valuable prelude to the individual interviews, allowing us to make the best use of the interview itself to focus on issues specific to that individual. The other slightly unusual aspect of our methods was the use of vignettes in the focus groups. What was unusual was that the vignettes were developed from the team members' own 'critical incident' diaries, so that we could feel confident that we were presenting vignettes that were grounded in their own experiences. Not only did this prove to be an effective research tool, but it was an opportunity for reflection that the team members seemed to welcome. It may be that this technique has further potential as a way of helping team members to explore their attitudes and beliefs in a relatively unpressured setting.

3

Organizing and managing multi-professional teams

David Cottrell

Introduction

In this chapter the functions and organizational structures of the five multi-professional teams participating in the MATCh research project will be outlined and analysed. Øvretveit (1993) examined multi-disciplinary teams working in adult mental health and as a result defined five organizational team types. This typology was helpful in our thinking about the organization of the teams in the study and we will apply it to them in this chapter. Figure 3.1 illustrates our thoughts on the different lines of accountability in multi-professional teams. The team types outlined by Øvretveit are as follows:

- *The fully managed team*: a team manager is accountable for all the management work and for the performance of all team members – see Figure 3.2.

- *The coordinated team*: one person takes on most of the management and coordination work but is not accountable for the clinical work of individual team members – see Figure 3.3.

- *The core and extended team*: the core team members are fully managed by the team leader with extended team members (usually part-time) remaining managed by their professional managers in their agency of origin – see Figure 3.4.

- *The joint accountability team*: most team tasks, including leadership, are undertaken by the team corporately, usually by delegating to individual members. Team members remain accountable to managers in their agencies of origin but in practice may not have strong management links with them – see Figure 3.5

- *The network association*: this is not a 'formal' team as such but different professionals working with the same client or client group meet together based on a need to share common work/clinical interests. Each practitioner remains under the management of their own professional manager but decisions about client care are often formulated collectively at network meetings.

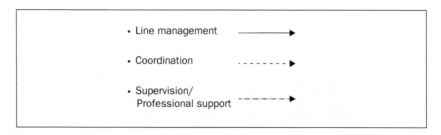

Figure 3.1 Key for lines of accountability

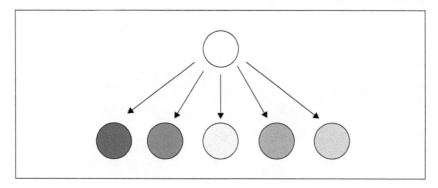

Figure 3.2 The fully managed team

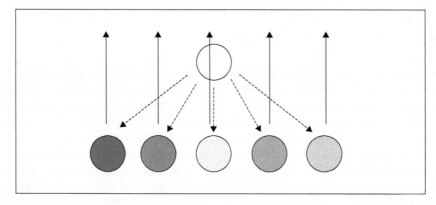

Figure 3.3 The coordinated team

All of the teams were based in the same city, some covering the whole of the city (and one, the neuro-rehabilitation team, covering the wider region). Two of the

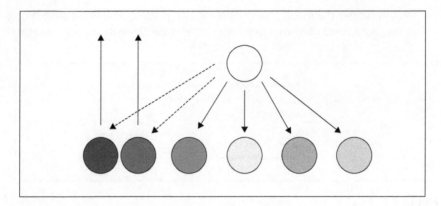

Figure 3.4 The core and extended team

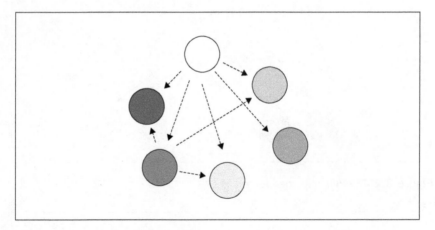

Figure 3.5 The joint accountability team

teams (youth crime and young people) covered just a sector of the city. Thus, all five teams offered services to the same sector of the city, although some offered services elsewhere as well. Given the (then) government's strategic intention to integrate children's services, as we outlined in Chapter 1, it is therefore not surprising that in interviews team members from one team made reference to the work of other teams participating in the research. It is possible to imagine a family where a younger child with a learning disability had been assessed by the child development team and attended the nursery and an older sibling who had suffered a head injury had behavioural problems, including offending behaviour that led to the involvement of the neuro-rehabilitation team, the young people's team and the youth crime team. Such a family would therefore have received services from all of our teams.

The functions, locations, membership and organizational structures of the teams are summarized in Table 3.1.

Table 3.1 Summary of team function, location, membership and organizational structure

Team function and size	Client group	Base	Lead sector	Agencies represented	Agency stakeholder liaison	Team type
Youth crime team (13 members)	Youth crime, 10–17 years	Independent community	Legal/police	Health, social services, education, police/probation, voluntary sector	Yes, partnership group	Fully managed
Young people's team (11 members)	Emotional and behavioural problems, 0–17 years	Social services, community	Social services	Health, social services	Yes, strategic development group	Fully managed*
Nursery team (11 members)	Learning disability, 0–5 years	Independent, community	Voluntary sector	Health, voluntary sector	No	Core (fully managed) and extended
Head injury team (13 members)	Traumatic brain injury, 0–17 years	Health, hospital	Health	Health, social services, education	No	Network/joint accountability
Child development team (14 members)	Learning disability, 0–5 years	Health, hospital	Health	Health, social services	No	Core and extended/joint accountability

*With exception of consultant clinical psychologist

The youth crime team

National policy at the time of the fieldwork

The development of youth offending teams can be traced back to the publication of the Audit Commission report *Misspent Youth* (1996). This report highlighted the lack of joined-up thinking within the youth justice system as a whole and a consequent inefficient deployment of resources, and in particular delay in the processing of youth offenders within the criminal justice system. The Crime and Disorder Act 1998 paved the way for the establishment of youth offending teams, whose principal aim was to reduce youth offending by children and young people (defined as those aged 10–17 years) in their area. The circular setting out the establishment of youth offending teams (Home Office 1998) specified that these teams should be multi-professional and should tackle factors associated with crime, such as poor parenting, abuse, mental health problems, truancy and substance misuse. The entire youth justice system was to be overseen by the Youth Justice Board, which sets the broad strategic and policy agenda for the youth justice system in England and Wales. The Act was fully implemented in April 2000. The teams, by statute, comprised at least one social worker, a probation officer and a police officer as well as persons nominated by the local health authority and local chief education officer. Funding for the team was from each of these agencies. In practice, teams tended to be larger and more multi-disciplinary than suggested by the statutory minimum. An Audit Commission report (2004) highlighted some of the ways in which the teams were operating well and also made suggestions to improve the functioning of the youth offending teams.

Local practice

The team that participated in this research served an area of large estates of former state housing and back-to-back or terraced housing. There were considerable pockets of deprivation in the area. The population of the former state housing estates might be described as white working class, while the private housing areas were lived in by families who had their origins in Pakistan or Bangladesh.

The team was located in an office block just south of the city centre. All the staff were based together in a building which had facilities for hosting meetings. Staffing at the time of the research comprised a manager, two social workers (youth justice officers), two probation officers, a police officer, a drugs worker, an education officer, a nurse and three youth support workers. Funding from agencies contributing to the team was in roughly the following proportions: social services, 55 per cent; probation, 20 per cent; police, 10 per cent; education, 10 per cent; and health, 5 per cent.

As shown in Figure 3.6, the team did not quite meet Øvretveit's (1993) criteria for a fully managed team. The manager, employed by social services, had line management responsibility for some aspects of staff employed by other agencies but team members still had functions line managed by managers within their

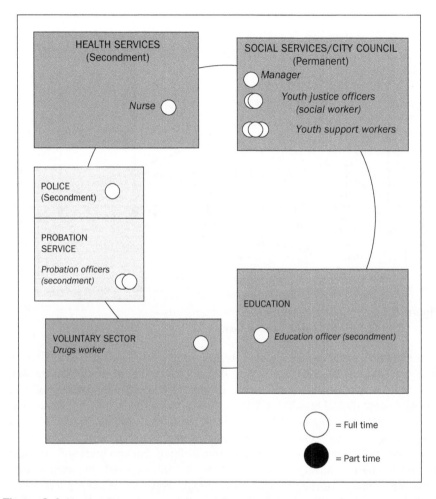

Figure 3.6 Youth crime team: employment structure

original agencies. The team was probably best described as a coordinated team, with the team manager having clear responsibility for ensuring that work was allocated according to agreed priorities (see Figure 3.7). As with all the youth offending teams in the city, the team was coordinated by a partnership group allowing the stakeholder agencies to have regular oversight of the team functioning.

The young people's team

National policy at the time of the fieldwork

In the early 1990s, concerns about the ad hoc and uneven nature of mental health services for children and families led to the NHS Health Advisory Service (HAS)

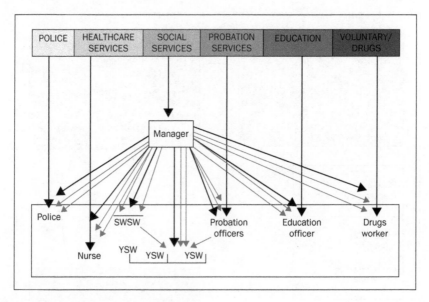

Figure 3.7 Youth crime team: management structure
(SW = Social worker; YSW = Youth support worker)

producing a thematic review, *Child & Adolescent Mental Health Services: Together We Stand* (NHS, HAS 1995). The review described the state of services at the time and made comprehensive recommendations for purchasers and providers of child and adolescent mental health (CAMH) services. A major theme was the requirement for joint commissioning and delivery of services across agencies. The multi-factorial aetiology of childhood mental health problems was seen as necessitating the involvement of a range of professionals from different backgrounds and therefore the collaboration of a range of agencies from the statutory and voluntary sectors. Adequate mental health services for young people were seen as having benefits for the future mental health of adults, but they would also impact on levels of child abuse, behaviour problems in schools, juvenile delinquency and family breakdown.

The HAS report proposed a tiered service model and was endorsed by the House of Commons Select Committee on Health in 1997. Tier 1 comprises front-line staff from a range of agencies (teachers, school nurses, general practitioners, health visitors, social workers) who have day-to-day contact with children with mental health problems but do not have specialist training in working with those problems. Tier 2 represents the first tier of specialist CAMH services. This comprises staff with specialist training in CAMH practice who, either singly or in teams, work in the community directly with children and families. They also provide consultation and training for Tier 1 staff to enable them to provide a better service for the children that they see on a daily basis. Tier 3 consists of teams of CAMH professionals working together to provide specialist interventions for complex problems. Tier 4 is the specialist provision of day and in-patient services.

Policy has reinforced the importance of multi-agency CAMH provision in the government's thinking about children's services (DfES/DoH 2004a). Multi-agency local delivery plans are now required to specify how improvements in CAMH services will be achieved and significant increases in expenditure are being delivered through local authority social services budgets as well as health, thus requiring health and social services to work together to deliver CAMH services. (For a history of CAMH services, see Cottrell and Kramm 2005.)

Local practice

In the city where the MATCh project took place there were at that time five community-based Tier 2 CAMH teams, two funded and managed by social services, with the other three teams funded and managed by health. All five teams worked to an agreed service description with common referral pathways and intervention packages. The teams were locally based, worked closely with other statutory and voluntary sector organizations within the local community, and acted as a first point of contact for anyone concerned about emotional and behavioural problems in children. The teams offered clinical/therapeutic interventions with children and families. They provided consultation, supervision, and training to Tier 1 professionals. They filtered referrals of a more complex and persistent nature to the Tier 3/Tier 4 CAMH teams.

The CAMH team in the MATCh project was originally based within a health centre but had recently relocated to a jointly funded (health and local authority) one-stop Children's Centre nearby. The team shared a building with local social service and primary care staff.

The staff group comprised a part-time manager and 8 generic child and adolescent mental health practitioners (CAMHPs), all employed by social services. This practitioner grade was a new one created for the purposes of establishing the team and allowed for people with a range of professional backgrounds (nursing, social work, occupational therapy) to be employed by social services on a single grade. The manager had full line management responsibility for these staff. A part-time consultant clinical psychologist and a senior CAMHP were seconded to the team from health. In addition, 2.5 school-based CAMHPs had temporary funding from the local children's fund (see Figure 3.8).

The team functioned as a fully managed team (Øvretveit 1993), as shown in Figure 3.9, except that the psychologist, who was line managed through health, had responsibility for clinical supervision within the team.

The nursery team

National policy at the time of the fieldwork

In the 1970s, educational provision for young children with disabilities moved from a 'medical model' where children were frequently assigned to residential

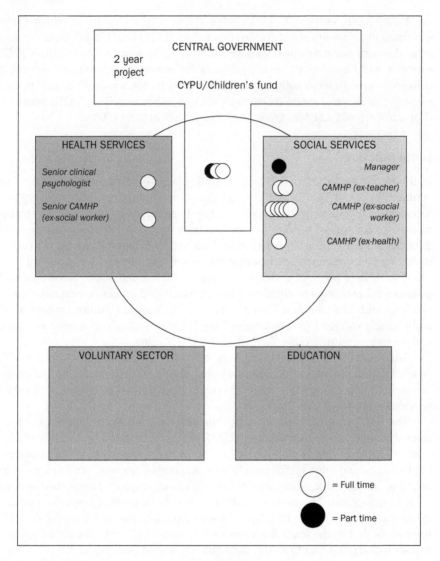

Figure 3.8 Young people's team: employment structure

schools away from their families, to a special school model where children were transported to local education authority provision. Special schools were categorized as for children with moderate, severe or severely subnormal learning difficulties. In the 1990s, there was a shift to an inclusion model where provision was within mainstream settings, sometimes as specialized units incorporated into primary school buildings. For children under 5, educational provision was incorporated into a diversity of settings: childcare, playgroups, nursery classes, nursery schools and Children's Centres. Some were financed

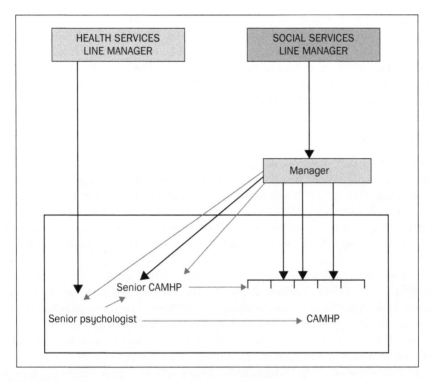

Figure 3.9 Young people's team: management structure

by local authorities and others by commercial interests or the voluntary sector (Wall 2003).

The seminal Warnock Report (DES 1978) had argued for a commitment to educating children with learning difficulties as a matter of right and for their needs to be assessed on a continuum. Education rather than health was to assume responsibility for identifying and assessing young children with special needs. Parents were to be closely involved as partners in decisions about provision. The Education Act (1981) provided a legislative framework to reflect these principles. Subsequently, the Children Act 1989 identified the need for multi-disciplinary approaches to providing services. The *Special Educational Needs Code of Practice* (DfES 2001) re-emphasized the importance of early identification, diagnosis and provision for children with learning disabilities and the importance of a multi-disciplinary approach to decision-making. There was a strong message about inclusion: wherever possible provision should be in mainstream settings. This resulted in a raft of special educational needs training for staff in mainstream pre-school and school settings, who were expected to respond to the needs of young children with a range of disabilities. In 2002, the Department for Education and Skills and Department of Health (DfES/DoH 2002a, 2002b) published guidelines for multi-agency working for the delivery of services to children with disabilities from birth to 2 and their families. Key messages in both documents were multi-agency assessment and decision-making, joint working, information-sharing and a child-centred approach to provision for young children with special needs. There was a pledge in the Children's Plan launched in 2007 that additional funding would be provided for children with special educational needs and children with dyslexia.

Local practice

The nursery that participated in the research had opened in 1963 operating under the auspices of the Royal Society for Mentally Handicapped Children and Adults (MENCAP). It was based in their main headquarters in a converted nursery school building. The nursery was a registered charity and there was a small daily charge for children's attendance. The nursery ethos dominated the building. Seconded health workers had rooms allocated for one-to-one work with children and parents.

The nursery offered services to 40 children with learning disabilities, from birth to 4, and their families. Referrals came from a wide range of sources across the city. Many of the children had additional (some multiple and profound) disabilities: physical, sensory and behavioural as well as developmental delay. Following enrolment, parents and nursery workers completed an integrated assessment leading to an individual education plan for the child. Provision for children included play-based learning activities, physiotherapy, speech therapy and organized visits to the library, shops, parks, local leisure centres and museums/galleries. Adults were offered group parenting and support sessions, sometimes with visiting speakers, and individual advice and counselling sessions. Health workers provided direct work with children and parents but were increasingly expected to 'train' nursery staff in their specialist knowledge/ expertise by modelling activities with children in the main classrooms. There was outreach work in family homes through the 'Portage' home visitor scheme. The training officer worked in a range of early years settings, mentoring mainstream staff in the skills and expertise of provision for young children with additional needs. Many of these initiatives were innovative in their time, and indeed the kinds of practices that were espoused by SSLPs in the first decade of the new millennium.

The staff group comprised a head of nursery, counsellor, senior nursery nurse, 3.5 nursery nurses, a nursery escort/assistant, an administrative assistant, an ethnic minority development worker, a minibus driver, cleaner and assistant cleaner, bookkeeper, fundraising and development manager and fundraiser as well as a Portage home visitor. Health staff with specific sessions allocated to the nursery included two part-time physiotherapists and one part-time speech therapist. In addition, a full-time training officer was funded by the local Early Years Development and Childcare Partnership (EYDCP), at that period the way in which funding was distributed to early years services within local authorities.

There were also a range of voluntary workers contributing to cooking, driving and working with the children. Funding came from three main sources: grants from the local education authority and NHS, fundraising from ongoing MENCAP systems, and donations (see Figure 3.10).

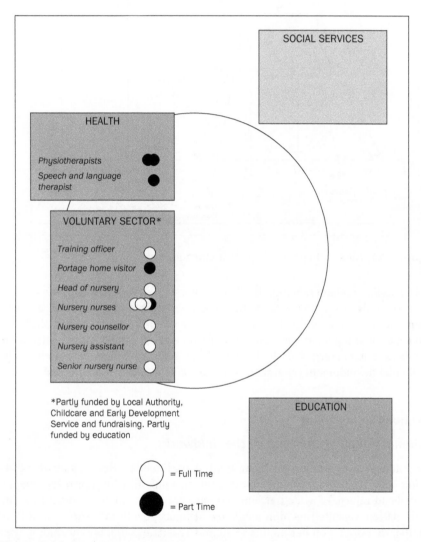

Figure 3.10 Nursery team: members employment structure

The nursery team, as shown in Figure 3.11, was best described as a core (voluntary sector) and extended (NHS) team. Within the core nursery team there was a clear hierarchy with strong leadership from the nursery head in the style of a fully managed team. NHS extended team members were managed by

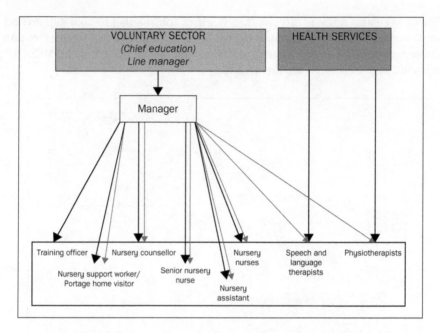

Figure 3.11 Nursery team: management structure

their own line managers within the NHS. A nursery advisory group was responsible to a chief executive who in turn was responsible to a board of trustees. There appeared to be little in the way of a formal relationship between MENCAP and senior management within the NHS responsible for the NHS extended team members, but nursery staff had strong links with other agencies such as the local child development team with whom we also worked in the project.

The head injury team

National policy at the time of the fieldwork

Head injury is a common problem, with Department of Health statistics indicating over 100,000 admissions to hospitals in England with a primary diagnosis of head injury, of which at least 30 per cent were children under 15 years (DoH 2001a). Despite this high incidence of injury, death rates are low at 6–10 per 100,000 population per annum (Kay and Teasdale 2001), but morbidity after injury is high and far exceeds the capacity of UK neuro-rehabilitation services. Nearly half of those surviving after head injury may have some form of restriction to lifestyle with severity of disability not necessarily related to severity of injury (Thornhill et al. 2000).

Despite this, there is a lack of coherent policy concerning the long-term care of children with acquired brain injury in the UK, although a number of evidence-based guidelines have been published on managing various aspects of head injury. In 2003, the National Collaborating Centre for Acute Care was commissioned by the National Institute for Clinical Excellence (NICE) to produce an evidence-based clinical guideline on the early management of head injury in children and adults (NICE 2003). The guideline offers 'best practice for the care of all patients who present with a suspected or confirmed traumatic head injury with or without other major trauma'. Where appropriate, separate advice is offered for adults and children but the guideline does not address the rehabilitation or long-term care of patients with a head injury. A guideline published jointly by the British Society of Rehabilitation Medicine (BSRM) and the Royal College of Physicians (RCP) later in 2003 (BSRM/RCP 2003) provided complementary advice on the longer-term rehabilitation of head-injured patients. Although the advice is aimed at adult patients, much of it is relevant for the rehabilitation of children.

Prior to this, the NICE guideline reported that the first UK-wide guidelines on identifying patients who were at high risk of intracranial complications following a head injury were drawn up by a working party of neurosurgeons in 1984 and used in the UK for over 15 years with subsequent modifications published by the Society of British Neurological Surgeons in 1998 and the Royal College of Surgeons of England in 1999. In 2000, the Scottish Intercollegiate Guidelines Network (SIGN) published a guideline on the early management of head injury that included sections relevant to the care of children.

It is of note that one of the 'exemplar patient journeys' that was published to support the National Service Framework (NSF) for children, young people and maternity services and to illustrate key NSF themes concerned acquired brain injury in children (DfES/DoH 2004b).

Local practice

The head injury team worked with children and young people admitted to hospital with moderate to severe traumatic brain injury. The hospital was a regional centre and patients were admitted from a wide area. The team provided initial acute care of the child and family in the immediate aftermath of the injury. It continued to work with the family through the rehabilitation phase for months or even years in severe cases.

Most team members were based in the acute hospital. There was no formal team base as team members had offices within their own departments in the hospital. Team meetings took place in a seminar room off the ward. The main geographical focus of work was in the neurological ward itself and to a lesser extent in the hospital school, and in the outpatient clinic. This clinic was located in the same building as the child development team with which we worked in the project. All team members had other core functions but contributed some sessions to neuro-rehabilitation. At the time of the research, the team comprised a consultant paediatric neurologist and sessional contributions from a consultant psychiatrist, consultant psychologist, occupational therapists, speech and language therapists, physiotherapists, nursing staff on the paediatric neurology ward, the hospital school teacher and a social worker (see Figure 3.12).

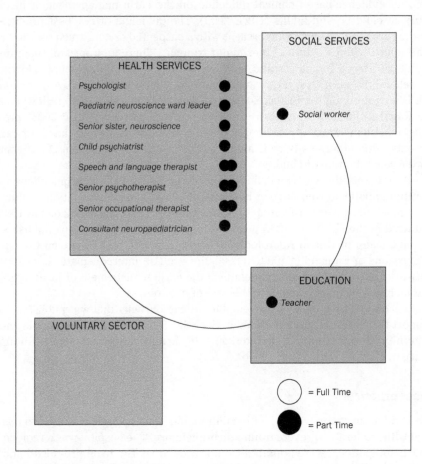

Figure 3.12 Head injury team: employment structure

The head injury team was best described as a network association of professionals from different backgrounds who came together because they had a common interest in coordinating the care of children with traumatic brain injury. There were no formal team/network meetings but all members met weekly as part of a larger paediatric neurology meeting that coordinated the management of all children with neurological problems in the hospital. Some internal leadership came from the consultant paediatrician but other senior team/network members also took on leadership roles for particular tasks. The team/network had regular, quarterly away days to discuss joint working, policies and procedures and to engage in team-building. As shown in Figure 3.13, there were no formal

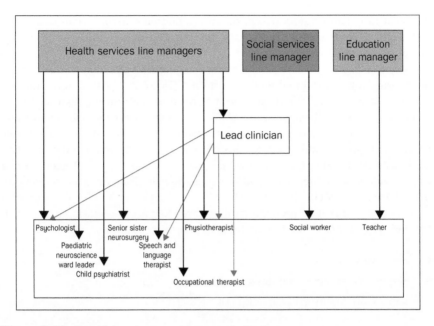

Figure 3.13 Head injury team: management structure

links between the stakeholder agencies employing the different team/network members.

The child development team

National policy at the time of the fieldwork

The Sheldon Report (1968) called for child assessment teams to be set up so that disabled children could receive more coordinated services (Hall 1997). The multi-agency approach was advocated to overcome the problem of families having to tell their stories repeatedly to different professionals, and experiencing gaps in service. The Court Report (DoH 1976) endorsed the child development centre offering assessment, therapy and treatment. It introduced the concept of district teams with both a clinical and managerial function. It envisaged child development teams staffed by paediatricians, nurses, social workers, psychologists and teachers (Hall 1997). Most child development teams cater for preschool children with cerebral palsy, severe learning disabilities and disabling communication problems such as autism and severe language impairment. There are marked variations in client groups and staffing mix in the UK, although most have been led by doctors (Bax and Whitmore 1991; Zahir and Bennet 1994).

In 2007, the Labour government published a crucial report with the ambitious aim of transforming the lives of disabled children. In many ways this was a typical New Labour initiative in terms of children – it was wide-ranging and ambitious, demonstrating a belief that the state can change the lives of children in a positive direction.

Aiming Higher for Disabled Children argues that disabled children should be seen as 'both a local and national priority' (DCSF 2007b: 6) and the minister admitted that disabled children 'have not been as high on the agenda as they should have been in the past' (Balls 2007). The target was established in the 2007 Children's Plan of achieving this transformation by 2011. The *Aiming Higher* report attempted to address the needs of: 'The 570,000 disabled children in England, around 100,000 of whom have complex care needs, [who] need support from a wide range of services, and so should be benefiting even more than most from these reforms' (DCSF 2007b: 11).

The *Aiming Higher* report identified three key areas requiring action if the outcomes for disabled children and young people were to improve:

- empowerment;
- responsive services and timely support;
- improving quality and capacity (DCSF 2007b: 5).

Local practice

The team was set up in 1990, following national good practice guidance, as part of disability services to serve sectors of the city. For many years, practitioners were employed by the local acute NHS trust but at the time of the project most practitioners in the team were employed and managed by local primary care trusts.

The team was based in a row of converted Victorian terraced houses adjacent to the acute hospital where paediatric services were provided. Accommodation was shared with a child protection team, a bereavement counselling service and a growth and nutrition team. The inside of the building was described by staff as a bit of a 'rabbit warren' and included narrow staircases, many small and large consulting rooms and offices at various levels, making disabled access difficult.

The centre assessed and provided services for mostly pre-school children aged 0–5. Referrals were from a wide range of sources, including GPs, health visitors, senior clinical medical officers in the community, speech and language therapists and a variety of acute hospital paediatricians. The range of disorders seen comprised: cerebral palsy; learning difficulties/developmental delay; a range of syndromes, including Down's; autism and complex communication disorders; profound multiple learning difficulties; dyspraxia; degenerative conditions; and sensory impairment. These can result in any combination of: feeding difficulties; gross motor difficulties; fine motor difficulties; delayed cognitive development; delayed/ disordered speech/language development; behaviour/relationship problems; social needs; equipment/aids and adaptations needs. Weekly multi-disciplinary assessments involved all team members and the child and family. Children were offered regular ongoing input from at least two members of the team.

At the time of the research the team was funded mainly by the NHS and comprised four paediatricians, a health visitor, two nursery nurses, a psychologist, two speech and language therapists, two occupational therapists, two physiotherapists and an administrator. In addition, a social worker funded by the local authority was seconded to the team (see Figure 3.14).

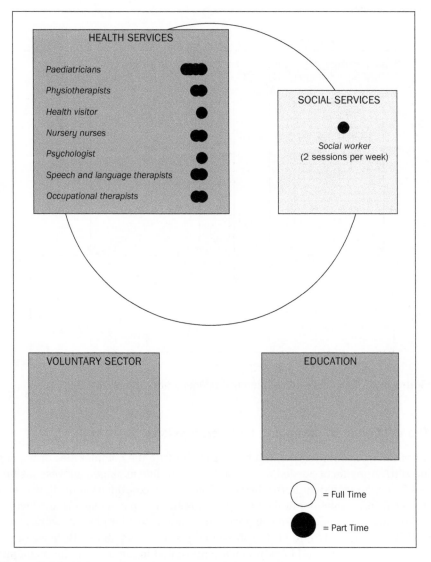

Figure 3.14 Child development team: employment structure

The child development team was closest to Øvretveit's (1993) core and extended structure with some team members having greater time commitments to the team than others. Although the consultant paediatrician was the designated team leader and had some team management/coordination responsibilities, other disciplines were line managed outside the team by their own line managers and took the lead on some areas of the team's work. The leadership style was 'hands off' and similar to a joint accountability team. As shown in Figure 3.15, there appeared to be few formal links between the different agencies that employed team members.

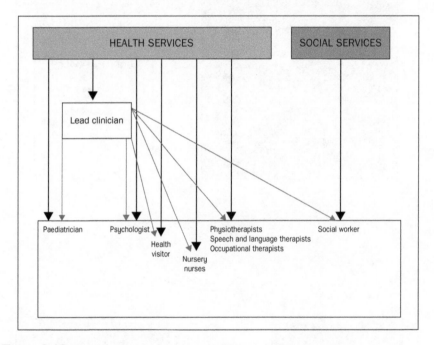

Figure 3.15 Child development team: management structure

The challenge of managing multi-professional teamwork

All of the teams in this research had struggled with the complexities of managing staff. Agreement needed to be reached about line management responsibilities (e.g. who would authorize leave and absence), coordination of the work of the team (e.g. which team member would take on a particular piece of work) and professional supervision/support (e.g. how a particular piece of work would be delivered according to best professional practice guidelines). Because of the wide range of skills and backgrounds represented in the team, team managers and leaders often found themselves unable to provide appropriate professional support or supervision to some team members and separate arrangements were made for this to be provided by someone more appropriate.

All the teams in our sample had developed complex structures to balance the demands of different agency stakeholders and team members – although seemingly straightforward issues were often more complex when examined closely. Thus, although in some teams the three functions of line management, coordination and supervision were delivered to some staff by the same person, it was not unusual to find a team member being line managed by one person (from their host agency), coordinated by a team leader and supervised professionally by a third person. Agencies often continued to take line management responsibility for their staff even when there was a person called a 'team manager'. Team managers often had direct line management responsibility for some staff (delegated from stakeholder agencies) but a more coordinating role for other staff.

It appeared that many of these issues had not been determined when the teams were first formed, but had developed in an ad hoc manner over time. It is noteworthy that three of the teams seemed to have no formal reporting links with the group of agencies that funded them and therefore had limited opportunities to discuss these issues. What was clear was that only the stakeholding agencies had the authority to make final decisions in these areas. The potential for teams to be distracted from their core tasks by the time spent on resolving management structures was significant. Practical problems concerning differences in pay, leave entitlements and freedom to make decisions without referral to line managers caused real problems for team members and their managers, who reported an adverse effect on morale. Observation of team meetings and documentation suggested that other structural issues such as part-time or full-time team membership and physical location of the team (and whether all team members shared a single base) also had a significant impact on team and individual functioning.

While there is probably no one correct organizational structure for multi-professional teams (Frost 2005), it is possible to suggest some basic requirements for teams to be able to function. All team members should have their work clearly coordinated with other members of the team. All team members need to have appropriate support for personal and professional development. Above all, team members need to have absolute clarity about who is performing each of these tasks for themselves and for their team colleagues. All agencies need to develop formal structures for liaison with other agencies responsible for a multi-agency team and to agree collectively about how the team and its members will be managed. These agencies all need clarity about the aims and objectives of the team if the team is to organize itself to deliver these objectives.

The teams in this study had themselves developed a number of joint activities to facilitate effective multi-professional working, with considerable time and effort going into team-building and team development activities. Participation in regular team meetings was prioritized and all of the teams used occasional away days to share ideas and develop new ways of working. Team meetings and away days usually included time for collaborative reflection and active exploration of diverse perspectives, often organized around case presentation and discussion. Teams often organized shared training and/or supervision events to provide further opportunities for developing shared working practices. The creation (reification) of shared protocols for assessment and intervention in different situations was another useful focus for team discussion and for the development of a shared language and terminology for describing and discussing team activities.

More informally, participation in everyday activities such as working together to conduct shared assessments or deliver joint interventions also helped to create and maintain a sense of 'tameness', as did casual 'coffee' or 'corridor chats'. All of these activities took time and yet seemed an essential part of creating a team that could function. The stakeholder agencies that supported these teams seemed to understand this and had allowed considerable time to be invested in activities that Øvretveit described as team nurturance and maintenance and that the members of these teams often described as building mutual respect and understanding.

Conclusion

In this chapter we have outlined the way the teams that participated in our study were organized and managed. Using Øvretveit's (1993) framework we have been able to provide a typology of team types. The national policy context at the time the research fieldwork was undertaken and the local practice of teams have been outlined and examined. We can now go on to outline and analyse the findings from our core MATCh study.

Part 2
Working and learning in a multi-professional team

This part of the book explores how professionals in multi-professional teams worked together and the implications of changes in their work for their professional ideologies, identities and learning.

4

Multi-professional perspectives on childhood

Mark Robinson, Angela Anning and Nick Frost

Introduction

It has become common to argue that social problems and indeed childhood itself are socially constructed (Jenks 1996; Frost 2011). The implication of social construction for this book is that the definition of the problems and challenges faced by children and their families is shaped by social forces and discourses – the problems do not exist independently of these discourses. While 'social construction' is an overarching social theory, in this chapter we are able to assess some of the minutiae of how social construction works in actual practice situations in the five teams included in the project.

Different professionals could be expected to construct 'their' service users within separate and, perhaps, competing discourses. These discourses become central to the ways professionals work together – or indeed fail to do so. We would argue that these constructions are central to the multi-professional agenda that we cover in this book. In this chapter we explore the many and complex issues to do with how the five multi-professional teams understood their work and defined the issues faced by children and their families.

Models of understanding utilized by professionals

In the fieldwork undertaken for the MATCh project we were able to gather a considerable amount of data relating to competing or complementary models used by professionals in the five teams. The evidence existed in relation to key issues such as assessment, defining need, predisposing factors, and current problems faced by children and their families. How did the different professionals construct and apply meaning to the situations they faced? As we have seen,

Wenger (1998) argues that meaning constructed through practice is central to building communities of practice.

All the teams shared what we might call complex models of understanding: we saw no evidence of crude, uni-causal or over-deterministic models. However, the teams had a tendency to hold a dominant model of explanation – although this dominant model was not always shared by the entire team, and was often accompanied by a secondary or complementary model of explanation.

These prevalent explanatory frameworks underlying practice for each team are shown in Table 4.1.

Table 4.1 The five team models of understanding childhood issues

Team	Dominant model	Complementary model
Young people's team	Family/systemic	Social deprivation
Child development team	Medical	Social/psychological support
Youth offending team	Social structural	Individual impact
Nursery team	Individual needs	Holistic approach
Head injury team	Medical	Social/psychological support

A systems approach

In the young people's team, the dominant approach was heavily influenced by systems theory. Throughout the period of data-gathering with this team the respondents made numerous references to how they understood the issues confronting them in terms of family functioning and systems-based approaches. The search for systemic explanations and underlying causes and meanings dominated their worldview. They believed that in order to fully understand family systems, careful assessment has to take place. A typical comment was: 'I mean, we use quite a standard assessment frame ... where the initial assessment will go through lots of aspects of family functioning and previous history, and significant events. And I suppose we are using some kind of family assessment model really.' This was a primary method of understanding the problems the team members confronted, but it is important to note that the teams also took into account the complex 'systems' within which families are located, including key social contexts such as schools, housing and peer groups. Family issues for this team thus have to be seen as part of a 'family system' situated in a network of wider systems.

The complexity of real-life problems made it difficult for agencies to target intervention. The use of this systemic approach by a team dedicated to improving children's psychological health led the team to dilemmas of identifying boundaries between agencies. A team member reported: 'A lot of families, I think, locate the difficulties purely within the children and in fact the issues are far more systemic and that generates huge issues for all agencies because there are so many families that could fall between everybody's camp.'

The model utilized by the young people's team conceived of social disadvantage as an influence on family behaviour, but applied a 'systemic' psychological model to assessment, foregrounding intervention at the family level. There was a view that social disadvantage influenced parental competence, as expressed by the following two respondents:

> And at heart they want to get it right, they love their kids, they want to be good parents to their kids but they don't actually have a model of how you do that.

> A family is in crisis, I guess, really. Some are in crisis because of just long-term social problems; social pressures, you know, living in a very run-down area with lots of crime; lots of drug dealing; parents who've come from a very difficult background.

Thus, while wider social factors were taken into account, the practical edge of the team led to an emphasis on issues which they could clearly address through their practice. We can note therefore a potential gap between theoretical explanations (e.g. social) and the practical techniques of actual intervention. This classic gap between professional 'espoused theory' and 'theory in action' (Argyris and Schön 1976) existed to some degree in all the teams we studied.

While structural disadvantage and a resulting impact on parenting competence were important, the approach of the young people's team was qualified by the team manager and the senior practitioner who focused on social competence. Asked to describe the group she worked with, the senior practitioner said: 'I think the majority of the families that I deal with are able to access services, are able to engage in verbal therapy, are able to engage in cognitive therapy, because I think that they do have the capacity to be able to benefit from that type of treatment.' Thus the socially constructed model of understanding – that problems exist in family systems – meant that families had to be motivated in exploring these through the largely verbal methods adopted by the team.

One of the senior clinical practitioners in the team reinforced this analysis by highlighting the use of assessment and intervention approaches based on a systemic psychological model that took account of wide-ranging social influences:

> So I tend to see problems in terms of systems as being within family systems and within wider systems, meaning I'll start with the family system but then that might also include the school system, or it might include the health system or the community. But that tends to be my perspective, I'm quite systemic in the way I view things.

The senior practitioner distinguished her approach from a typical medical model, however, because her construction of problems did not locate diagnosis and intervention in the individual: 'It really was not individual therapy. The medical model tends towards an individual diagnosis. It was very systemic.'

A medical model

In the child development team we studied, all respondents saw their practice as being based primarily on medical diagnosis. They complemented medical and practical resource interventions with the psychosocial support they offered.

A difference between this model and that used by the young people's team we have already discussed was that the starting point was the medical diagnosis of the child and/or the systems. As a result, the parents might be viewed as potential 'victims' of the actual condition and the stigmatizing tendencies in society. Like the respondents from the young people's team, the child development practitioners saw parents as the main client group. A typical comment was: 'The overall client group are really the parents and carers, caregivers, of children with developmental disorders and disabilities, but also it is the actual children, but one does work more directly with the adults involved than actually with the child.' They also expressed commitment to a model of partnership with parents:

> We're still changing partly in response to the knowledge but also partly in terms of moving further down the idea of working in genuine partnership with families which we've always thought we were doing, that kind of thing, but there's always more you can do.

> You do get involved in the emotional side of things for parents coming to terms with their child's disability or their delay; but you do the emotional as part of the practical, you know, you can go in to do a home visit to focus on something practical and spend the session sitting talking about a parent's feelings about the child and how they're adapting to the child's situation.

A similar medical/psychological model was observed in the head injury team with medical diagnosis triggering interventions responsive to the psychological consequences of traumatic injury for children and their families. As one of the therapists explained:

> Usually they have had some acquired brain injury, either from a road traffic accident or an acute bleed or stroke as it's more familiarly known. So it's often quite, can be quite, stressful for the family and the child because obviously they were functioning 'normal' to this point and then suddenly parents and the child have had to experience intensive care.

The doctor in the team recognized the wider implications of a medical diagnosis: 'Everything from medical problems through to behavioural, cognitive, emotional, psychological, schooling, home, housing, family, family issues and problems will change depending on the age of the child.'

Respondents from a health background in this team emphasized a blend of medical intervention with psychological counselling and resource support. However, a psychologist in the team also highlighted the issues from their professional perspective: 'Stigma, impaired personal functioning, management of uncertainty, managing recovery, not just going through recovering process but managing your recovery process.' Here the same respondent reflects some of the views that we have seen are espoused in the young people's team we have already analysed: 'I think some of them are within individuals, but I think many of them are sort of, what I call systemic. Schools have to then manage a different pupil, or teach a different pupil to the one that they had previously.'

Again we noted that teams did not always share a universal worldview. The head injury team social worker claimed that consultants attached to the team followed a dominant medical model, whereas she applied a social model:

> Whereas I will get to know a family ... I will talk to the parents, I will be able to talk to them about their other child, first name, you know 'how did he get on?', the consultants are really only interested in that child and their rehabilitation. And so what is success measured by really, is it by physical fitness, or is it about the child being able to successfully re-join the family and the family being able to care for the child in the community or whatever? So, it depends what aspects, what models you are working with really, whether it is the medical model or the social model.

As in the young people's team, two models seem to be able to exist alongside each other – with complementary aspects – but also with some tension.

A needs-based model

In the nursery team, where all the children had special needs, there was an emphasis on the individual and unique situation faced by each child and their family: 'You see them as an individual rather than a child with special needs, so really you just deal with it as normal really, not as anything different.' Referring to her service users, another member of the team put it like this, empathizing with the perspective of the child: 'I have needs and those needs need to be met as well you know. I am a child first and foremost, but I have some individual needs.' This stress on individuality was combined with a holistic emphasis on health-related psychological and social influences on preschool education. The importance of the family was highlighted, since the model involved parents in attending the educational setting regularly, and also involved counselling. However, the primary focus of intervention remained the individual child.

The individual needs model occurred in a context where professionals expressed fears that mainstream settings might to some degree ignore the individuality of children with special needs. A staff member viewed parents/carers as coming from different social and personal backgrounds with varying needs. This mirrored her insistence that the children were all different and they each had specific needs: 'It's trying to remember that they aren't professionals now. They're now parents. And then at the other end of the scale we've got people with learning difficulties who are now parents. And again they're going to need quite a bit of support in the home.' This model, therefore, has a strong focus on individual needs and the uniqueness of these needs – the systemic or social perspectives are relatively absent.

A social model

In the youth crime team a social model was most influential in enabling the team to understand and intervene with young offenders. When asked to define their client group, typical responses from this team were:

> If they have experienced disadvantage in any shape or form, throughout their younger life – and that could be developmentally, or financially, or physically, or emotionally – all those factors will predispose a young person to have mental health issues, or have limited resources to deal with stresses in life.

> Generally from working-class backgrounds. Nearly always poorly educated, either excluded from school or dropped out of school.

> Predominately white which is quite surprising given [where] we work ... but predominantly white, maybe 85–90 per cent white.

> I have yet to have young middle-class well-educated offenders with 'A' levels and degrees going out committing minor offences, whatever it may be, public order offences or what have you. All my client group, 95 per cent of my client group, have been, as you described, excluded, come from excluded backgrounds.

Here then, social class, exclusion and poverty predominate. However, this dominant social model contrasted with the superficially similar emphasis on social influences we have already outlined in the young people's team. In the youth crime team, influences on social exclusion were viewed as key determinants, whereas in the young people's team, social factors were seen as mediated through family systems and perceived to be key determinants of a child's emotional health.

In the youth crime team, the 'strong' version of the social model applied by the probation officer led to him asserting that psychological problems were almost not a factor at all:

> But I think that's largely because 95 per cent of the people I see fit into the deprivation/economic exclusion model ... I've had may be one person who's got psychiatric/psychological problems since I've been here ... the overwhelming bulk of young people we see have very, very, very similar problems; it's drug use, it's exclusion ... there's no discussion around that.

However, these 'strong' versions of the social explanatory model existed alongside more multi-causal and complex explanatory versions within the youth crime team. The model as applied by the respondents did not imply that the children were all 'innocents'. They were seen as quite possibly 'damaged' by the impact of social disadvantage and exclusion. Here a 'pathology' model of 'damage' existed in a complex interplay with social forms of explanation.

Application of a 'strong' explanatory social model could lead to tensions. For example, one of the health-based members of the team was leading the team to increase its capacity to carry out baseline mental health assessments and conduct anger management sessions in response to a growing emphasis on mental health issues from the Youth Justice Board. This member of staff made links between this dominant model and a complementary model – where the 'social' model had 'individual' consequences.

The team manager suggested that predisposition or vulnerability to social disadvantage could occur in young people with weakened family support networks, again making links between the social model and individual impact on clients:

> A lot of them don't have any parents by the virtue of the fact that they're estranged from them, or they have sort of step-parents or they've moved into care settings. And I think those kids are very, very disadvantaged ... a very disadvantaged group and they tend to lack in schooling, lack in general ability, and they tend to be much more caught up in street culture, peer-group pressure and so on.

Strongly held views on the social explanatory model existed alongside these complex versions. However, the social model prevailed, and its practical application and explanatory relevance were exemplified by the comments of a drugs worker. For her, young people were viewed in as non-judgemental a way as possible: 'You've got to approach each individual as not one specific fault-finding exercise. There are so many things that can contribute and can build up and escalate into something that's quite devastating in this young person's life, and it's going to affect them always.' She argued that these young people's lives were in chaos due to forms of social disadvantage impacting on them, combined with their own flawed coping strategies:

> It's chaotic in that there could be community issues, such as antisocial behaviour, allegations, so that's at community level, the social services' involvement ... which may involve some form of neglect or abuse of the young person. So that would add to the chaos. And then, on top of that, you've got the escapism, which may involve using drugs or solvents or substances to try and escape their existence.

The intervention stance adopted by this practitioner was underpinned by a model in which offending was influenced by stigmatizing and disadvantageous social factors. The stance is best illustrated by the following statement: 'They don't ever come to me as a drug user, they come to me with a vulnerability to drugs issues. Because if we label them, they can become it [that label].'

Professional models of understanding

In all the five multi-professional teams we found weaker and stronger versions of the prevalent model held by different team members or utilized at different moments by the same person. We should not imagine therefore that professional identities give rise to universally fixed or shared explanatory models. The existence of internal variations in explanatory models suggests that there are dilemmas for our teams in achieving cohesion, through negotiating shared practice models, while at the same time embracing and celebrating complexity and diversity.

A challenge for all multi-professional teams is to reflect together on the models underlying their practice engagement with service users. These models are theoretical – in the sense that they are abstracted from a range of learning and experience – but they also need to 'work' in the sense that they are practical working ideologies that have to be applied in practice in everyday settings.

For all our teams, shared expertise was required to assess problems according to various criteria of complexity, in order, for example, to develop appropriate levels of intervention and to filter referrals. Part of the complexity faced by multi-professional teams was that, while they use shared expertise to assess service users on the basis of categories of complication, chronicity and severity, they were still constrained by remits, resources and prevailing models so that they were unable to deal with all facets themselves. Each team was therefore part of a web and network of resources that had a profound impact on their practice.

Conclusion

In summary, different multi-professional teams have differing modes of explanation – and these modes can exist in the same team at different times and with a differing emphasis.

What does all this mean for integrated forms of working? We regarded all the teams we explored as functioning well, as exhibiting high standards of practice and as practising to differing degrees as 'communities of practice' (Wenger 1998). Our data suggest that teams and professionals can work together, utilizing differing models of explanation. Indeed, it may well be the case that service outcomes are improved with flexible and responsive modes of explanation.

Our evidence was that 'social construction' became a reality through the workings of the teams in the MATCh project. They socially constructed the problems of the families they worked with through the exercise of a professional 'gaze'. The 'gaze' generated models of explanation that impacted on their modes of practice, treatments and interventions. Some of the policy and practice implications of this chapter will be considered in the next three chapters of this book.

Think points

Examine the explanatory models outlined in Table 4.1.

- Do you have an explanatory model that you adhere to?
- Is there a dominant model in your work/placement setting?
- What issues/challenges arise from people holding differing explanatory models?

5

Changing roles and responsibilities in multi-professional teams

Mark Robinson, Angela Anning and Nick Frost

Introduction

In Chapter 3, we investigated how the organization and management of structural aspects of the five multi-professional teams impacted on the way they operated. We considered how systemic and structural aspects of teamwork constrained or facilitated individual team members in their daily work. In Chapter 4, we explored the explanatory beliefs and values that underpinned whole-team activities. We gave some examples of how dominant and subsidiary models existed side by side and showed how individual professionals worked at reconciling their own beliefs and value systems with those dominating their team culture. In this chapter we will explore how the professionals responded to changes in roles and responsibilities within team activities and what impact these changes in their working lives had on their professional identities. We regard challenges and shifts in professional identities as a central aspect of working in multi-professional teams.

Developing a sense of who we are, in particular in relation to how those around us perceive us (Harré 1983), forges our personal identities. How we are positioned within families – for example, as the 'baby' of the family or 'the pretty one' – has a huge impact on our sense of self or identity. In turn, our identity affects what we think we are able to do. It guides our orientation to the world around us and determines the kinds of choices we make about our participation in the world. For example, if a child's identity includes a belief that they are good at learning, they will persevere with activities that seem difficult, confident that they are more likely than not to find a way to do them. They are likely to enjoy and benefit from learning opportunities rather than dread them. Sometimes a traumatic event, such as a breakdown in family life, or a major health problem, will destabilize a hard-won sense of who we are. Such events may cause an individual to work towards a different identity – perhaps less sure of their capabilities, maybe more determined to overcome disabilities. So identity formation involves learning to be yourself through a complex interplay of personal histories and societal expectations. In the modern world these identities are often complex, shifting and fluid (Jenkins 2002).

So it is with professional identities. As Wenger (1998) argued, a community of practice works at two levels. At the first level, each individual member brings to the community a sense of professional identity derived from their own working history, knowledge and expertise. These individual histories and knowledge bases contribute to the potential richness and capacity of the community of practice. Identity is one of Wenger's four main organizing concepts in his model of a community of practice, alongside meaning, practice and community. As we suggested in Chapter 1, for Wenger (1998: 5), identity is changed by both personal and social experiences in the workplace.

At a second level, the community has a corporate history and culture derived from the daily working activities of the team as an entity. Members of teams are dependent on each other as they engage in activities in the workplace. Wenger wrote: 'Practice resides in a community of people and the relations of mutual engagement by which they can do whatever they do … Membership is a matter of mutual engagement. That is what defines a community' (1998: 74).

In this chapter we will illustrate some of the processes of changing roles and identities in integrated services for children by drawing on examples from the MATCh project. Engaging with the community of practice of a multi-professional team gives professionals new opportunities. We can create personal/professional histories of becoming someone who works in a different way and knows different things. We can learn to transform our professional identities as we take on new roles and responsibilities. However, these transformations may be painful. Our professional identities may be destabilized as we grapple with new roles and unfamiliar activities. For some professionals the pain of losing a professional identity built up over years of working in single agency contexts proves not to be worth the gain of finding a different, extended identity in a multi-professional team.

The then contemporary policy context provided by *Every Child Matters* (DfES 2003) and the Children Act 2004 has profound implications for professional identity. As British child welfare policy moved towards integration, professionals faced profound shifts and challenges in terms of their sense of personal identity. These changes in their working lives, and the effects on their ability to work effectively in the new climate of interagency collaboration, are inevitably influenced by their personal histories, their social class and their gender. Hall (1997) has explored how these historical factors impact on the way health workers cope with the processes of multi-professional teamwork.

In Chapter 2, we described the research methods we used to explore multi-professional teams at work. At the beginning of the project we analysed documents given to us by the teams which described their aims, structures and functions. We wanted to explore the interplay between what was set down on paper and evidence of the realities of their workplace activities. So we observed and took detailed notes on what happened at two of the teams' regular meetings. We then used this evidence to ask about working realities for key members of each team at one-to-one interviews. We asked them about the interplay between the evidence we had collected regarding roles and responsibilities within their teams as defined on paper and as exemplified in their daily situated workplace activities.

The first half of the chapter will explore the insights we gained into what child-focused professionals actually do, and how this has changed: 'what I do'. The second half will explore the effect of these changes in roles and responsibilities on people's sense of professional identity: 'who I am'.

What I do

Example 1: the youth crime team

The employment and line management structures for the youth crime team were described in Chapter 3. The team consisted of social workers, a probation officer, a police officer, generic workers called youth support workers and persons nominated by the health authority and chief education officer. Their principal professional role and responsibility as a team was 'the prevention of offending by children and young people' (aged 10–17 years).

In this team, weekly team meetings were held around an oval table in the spacious team meeting room. The meetings had formal agendas and were chaired and minuted by team members. Meetings consisted of procedural/team management items, opportunities for open discussion of cases, and team professional development slots, sometimes with guest speakers. However, agenda items were often imposed by external requirements from central government or local authority edicts addressing youth crime issues.

Figure 5.1 is an example of how we recorded seating arrangements and sequences of turn-taking regarding key decision-making at team meetings.

Below is the agenda for the particular meeting we are using here as an example of the processes of the youth crime team decision-making:

- meeting calendar;
- holiday cover;
- intensive supervision and surveillance programme liaison;
- referral order developments;
- effective practice meeting notification;
- specialist information/feedback;
- training notification – mental health awareness;
- case discussion;
- administration issues.

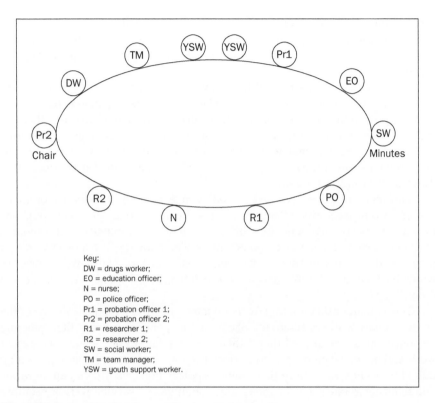

Figure 5.1 Seating plan for youth crime team meeting

We offer this example because Item 4 (referral order developments), the substantive agenda item of the meeting, illustrates a classic example of the blurring of professional roles and responsibilities in teams where workplace activities previously deemed to be the preserve of (qualified) specialists are assigned to (less qualified) generalists.

Overall in the meeting many team members contributed to the discussions during their allotted item on the agenda, and during the case discussions, though the short-term cover and agency staff said little. One of the generic youth support workers contributed substantially to discussions on pay/responsibility issues, and on case discussion, while the other was quieter. The team manager, though not chairing the meeting, tended to lead discussions. He presented, packaged in a positive way for the context of this multi-professional team, decisions taken at local authority level in an attempt to win support for his preferred (or imposed on him by external forces) course of action.

As mentioned, referral order developments were the main agenda item. The team manager was mediating decisions about role changes from outside the team by a citywide senior management team with overall responsibility for youth crime. The proposal was that management should transfer responsibilities for referral orders, traditionally held by specialist social workers or probation officers, to the generic youth support workers. However, the additional responsibilities were not to be recompensed by increases in pay to the youth support workers.

The team manager's preamble involved praising the team, especially the youth support workers, for doing excellent work. He explained that a local authority senior management team had decided that from now on referral orders were to be handled totally by the support workers. A new layer of external management, 'practice managers', was to be involved in supervision of the new arrangements. He assured everyone that the local authority felt confident that 'this was the right way forward'.

The team response seemed muted with a variety of low-key opinions voiced. A representative from education commented that the team could see the change as positive. A health worker asked how it would affect the support workers' current roles and responsibilities. The manager's response was that they would still do selective work on supervision orders, but their first priority would be dealing with referral orders, which they had demonstrated they could do well.

The manager asked for any further comments. After a long pause, one of the youth support workers spoke up. She raised key concerns about their pay and responsibilities. She argued that if they were starting to undertake assessment work and being asked to take total responsibility for a case, including for anything that went wrong, both these new responsibilities justified a pay increase. The manager replied that payment and conditions of service were a separate issue to be resolved in a local authority setting. He could not be responsible for this. His concern was for the distribution of work within the team, but not for individuals' pay and conditions. But he reassured the youth support worker that responsibility for referral orders overall was still to be overseen by a 'qualified' person, the practice manager, so there would be a support system for them in assuming these new responsibilities.

Teams as communities of practice (Wenger 1998) need cultural resources or 'coping strategies' to contain the tensions arising over policy-driven changes affecting working practices, roles and responsibilities. Shared cultural understandings need to be reached concerning both the purposes of change and the efforts being made within the team to ensure that professional standards are maintained while professional identities and needs are respected. The youth crime team membership represented diverse roles and professional backgrounds. As we pointed out in Chapter 3, their line management was often from outside the team. Inevitably, given their primary affiliations to mainstream outside agencies, there were differences in the way individual members were affected by proposed changes in working conditions and related pay, their roles as generalists or specialists, and their own career and personal aspirations. The silences we observed were sometimes as telling as what was spoken. Often the body language of team members told us much more than their words.

The relative quietness of some professionals in this episode could be viewed as strategic. No doubt they were weighing up potentially conflicting concerns. It is likely that individual professionals would be planning to advance their own interests 'off-stage', away from the public arena of the team meetings.

We were of course able to explore these conflicting views in the private spaces of the one-to-one interviews with team members when we asked them to comment on decisions we had seen made at meetings. As the interview extracts discussed below demonstrate, many of the youth crime team members did indeed have strong and conflicting views on these proposed changes in responsibilities for referral orders. A youth support worker felt that the policy change was potentially an opportunity for her to get paid for taking on new responsibilities, as reflected in the following quote: 'I think it's something we were doing anyway and we've been recognized for it. There's all the political stuff of job descriptions we're having to go into which is looking more muddy the further we go into it.' A social worker was optimistic and believed that the management had already addressed the youth support workers' concerns over pay and responsibilities: 'the management are backing them on the regrading claim and everything should be hunky-dory'. At the same time she saw difficulties in that: 'Support workers are at varying levels of ability and confidence. There's obviously going to be a changeover period.' She was also worried about the prospect of creating another layer of managers, in employing the proposed 'practice manager': 'It does leave certain questions still to be answered, yes, because the management team is still the largest in the city and it's getting larger.'

Team members who were employed by agencies and worked for the youth crime team through partnership agreements or secondment reported that they were frequently caught up in boundary disputes at local authority level about changes in professional roles and responsibilities. For example, a drug worker in the team, who regarded herself as a specialist, was asked to assume case management responsibilities. She regarded the practical problems as daunting. During her interview she told us that when she test-managed a case she 'didn't have the knowledge that was needed to address the whole thing'. Moreover, she explained to us that if she renegotiated her workload and pay for the time she spent working for youth crime teams, it would have implications for parity with other drug treatment workers working alongside her in her voluntary organization team. The impact of the complexity of the employment and management structures within the youth crime team was illustrated by the drug worker's dilemma here. She was juggling with the demands of two line managers and reflected that: 'The [youth crime] team supervision is about the individuals I am working with, and the … [voluntary agency] supervision is about the services I am offering and the manner in which I am offering that service.'

There were further themes of loss of autonomy and threat to identity for specialists as well as the practical problems generated by changing working practices. A specialist nurse, seconded from the health sector into the team led by social services, had resisted management attempts to make her take on a generic case management role in the team. Her struggle for autonomy was related to her perception of the team culture as 'a very strong social services culture that dominates', 'for example, the belief that although I was a nurse, I should have generic responsibilities'. Extracts from her interview illustrate a robust stance when faced with the imperative to assume generalist roles and responsibilities: 'I don't do any generic work at all, and so all the work that I do is around health issues to do with young people'; 'Yes, I am a nurse, I don't write reports for court. Only stuff to do with health.' There was antipathy to the idea that specialists within teams should not still be respected, each contributing particular strengths to the team's overall coordinated work activities. For example, a probation officer said: 'There was an idea in the probation service a few years ago, before my time, that, you know, you could do everything. That you were a mental health worker; you were a drugs worker, an alcohol worker. It's only nonsense.' A social worker also argued: 'If you're going to be involved in the life of other people, then the idea of the social worker being generic, all things to all people, should be dead in the water. Unfortunately it isn't at the moment. But certainly in our team that sort of approach has no currency.'

The youth crime team manager faced the unenviable challenge of retaining support across the team for changes imposed on him from above. Changes to one set of roles involved reshaping working practices for the entire team, and sustaining a vibrant and healthy culture, 'a culture of let's do it' and 'a heady brew' as he described it. At the same time, success in creating a new community of practice also depended on responding to the challenge of nurturing the individual professional identities of his staff. He knew that effective management was about 'the value put on people'. He believed that although the need for flexibility in changing roles and responsibilities could threaten professional identities and roles, changes also opened up for them new possibilities for learning. But he acknowledged that inevitably team members would see themselves as winners or losers. However, he was confident that the team was functioning well: 'Their cultural norms that they brought with them, have changed over a period of time. They've modified them ... and they've absorbed themselves into a multi-agency culture.'

Example 2: the young people's team

As we have seen, the young people's team was a community-based Tier 2 CAMH team managed by social services. Unlike the youth crime team, the initiative had been piloted by a group of professionals committed to changes in CAMH practices, rather than in response to a government requirement. Overall the team had far more autonomy than the youth crime team. The team employment structure was discussed in Chapter 3. Most staff members were employed by social services. A clinical psychologist and senior practitioner were employed by health. The team appointed generic CAMHPs with a variety of backgrounds, for example, nursery nurses, health visitors or youth workers.

Routine team meetings were held fortnightly in a meeting room with coffee and fruit provided. A typical seating plan is shown in Figure 5.2. Though meetings

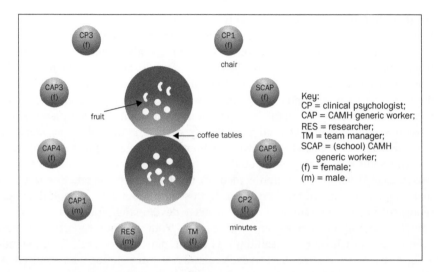

Figure 5.2 Young people's team seating plan for meeting

were structurally similar to those of the youth justice team (procedural/team management items followed by open-ended discussion and team development work), the young people's team meetings were freer to focus on business generated from within the team priorities. Below is the agenda for the young people's team meeting:

- minutes of last meeting;
- digital camera (office thefts);
- Tier 3 pilot (Tier 2 input to new referrals management procedures);
- case file audit;
- CH (new person to come);
- 'best' update;
- CAMH strategy/Tier 2 development (strategy discussion);
- cognitive behavioural treatment;
- new premises;
- courses.

The manager told the researcher that hers was a 'democratic' team and this gave the team 'energy'. The meeting was characterized by episodes of vigorous negotiation and debate (e.g. concerning the new referrals procedures item) and imaginative discussions of strategic options for the future (such as CAMH strategy/Tier 2 development). Two team members carried out minute-taking and chairing duties. The manager tended to lead discussions on organizational/procedural issues, but the clinical psychologist led the discussion on CAMH strategy. In this team, contributions were more evenly spread across the team. Even so, some members remained silent for much of the meeting.

Despite their perceived autonomy, the team was also subject to imperatives from national and local authority policies. For example, an internal memorandum from the department of social services within the city council, written by the children's service manager, had been circulated to the team. A citywide 'case file audit' had been carried out during the previous month. The audit had identified that not all assessments and intervention plans were recorded on the obligatory standard file. The manager reported that more assiduous record-keeping was demanded.

The audit report also included the requirement that in 'Case closure, each closed case should be seen and signed off by the team manager.' She stressed that they had no option but to respond to this central demand, though the audit report seemed to leave some room for teams to develop their own strategies as to how they should do so. She pointed to extracts from the audit report: 'The team need to decide whose responsibility it is to outcome the referral.' 'Team standards: is an assessment required on each case? Is the intervention plan required on all cases? If not, where will the team record their plan of work?'

There was a lively discussion about how the team should respond to the citywide imperative. Different viewpoints crystallized around their shared opposition to changes imposed on the team by outsiders. The imperative for case closures to be ticked off by the manager in a centralized way was most fiercely contested. It just did not fit with their culture of 'democracy'.

Social services were 'blamed' for demanding overzealous record-keeping. It was clear that the young people's team perceived themselves as distinct from social services, with different approaches to, for example, child protection. A social services worker mentioned fear of courts as a reason for recording practices, but the psychologist argued that there was a one in a thousand chance of court procedures. Another team member said this type of record-keeping was 'foreign to the culture' of people from a health background. It was also pointed out that social services did not offer the safeguard of clinical supervision in its working practices, whereas their team did. The psychologist argued that they were 'autonomous practitioners', but that she would agree to conform to the directive by paying it 'lip-service'. The manager offered a more conformist line, stressing that the team was located within the social services structure. She conceded that the new procedure would involve her in more work, but for her it was a 'safety issue' and it 'safeguards me'. As she pointed out, 'When things go less well with a practitioner, I have to be accountable.'

The debate raged on about the relative merits of health approaches to work, where 'you don't have to do what a supervisor says', and what was perceived as the bureaucratic practices of social services where 'if it's not written down, it hasn't happened'. One of the generic workers, in fact with a social worker background, responded robustly that the children's services manager was 'treating us like babies' and 'infantilizing us'. Finally, the manager tried to resolve the argument by providing a rationale, arguing that 'to help practitioners' there is a need for 'recording'. If an issue was not written down, things could go 'pear-shaped'. It was a 'management' issue not a 'case' issue that the team needed to keep a record 'for each child'. Pragmatically, she drew the discussion to a close by asking for a group of volunteers to create their own team case file document which would enable them to comply with the citywide imperative on recording and monitoring cases. Several colleagues agreed to do so.

Resolving conflict over the external (social services) decision to impose changes in the way they kept records generated considerable 'emotional labour' for members of this team. A newly appointed practitioner sat quietly, but at a critical point of the discussion pointed out that the proposals might be a 'waste of time' regarding 'accountability', but not regarding 'quality control'. She adopted a mediating role between the strikingly opposed positions taken by other team members. In her interview, she told us that her background as a trained psychotherapist enabled her to assess group dynamics within the team and reframe discussions to facilitate group processes and decision-making.

The very nature of their professional focus on psychotherapy and mediation made this team a particularly cohesive group. But relying on emotional bonds within the team culture could also lead to glossing over strong professional differences between practitioners. The team manager admitted in interview to the challenges of management, where both personalities and professional differences had an impact on the team's decision-making about 'what I do': 'Our styles can be quite different. We end up complementing each other but also sometimes have to think right, OK, where are each other's perspectives? And how do we dovetail them?'

Emergent themes

A number of themes about the implications of working in a multi-professional team emerged from our discussion of 'what I do':

- changes in roles and responsibilities affecting what they did were the catalyst for professionals' concern about parallel changes in their pay and conditions;
- professionals were sometimes caught up in 'boundary' disputes between agencies about what their training and background qualified/equipped them to do;
- professionals with specialist knowledge and expertise were unhappy about being 'rebranded' as generalists who could and should do everything;
- professionals were sometimes required to implement systems and procedures enforced by outsider or dominant agencies which seemed culturally unacceptable to them.

For managers, each shift in what a group of professionals were asked to do had implications for every other professional in their team.

Thus we can see that developing multi-professional teams is challenging and leads to many complex dilemmas – not all of which can be foreseen and planned for in advance.

Who I am

We turn now to evidence of changes in professionals' sense of 'who I am'. Frost (2005: 11) explores the concept of what it is to be a professional in the twenty-first century. He refers to the complex division of labour in modern society with its strata of workers based on the focus and orientation of their work; underpinning ideologies and technological/knowledge base; orientation towards clients; and status/prestige. He cites a definition of professionalism by Sims et al. (1993) as:

- a systematic body of knowledge and monopoly of powers over its applications;
- a self-regulating code of ethics, emphasizing values such as respect for the confidentiality of the client;
- the sanction of the community at large;
- control over the profession's own qualification and entry procedures;
- an altruistic orientation.

Bligh (in Petrioni 1994) described each profession behaving like a tribe, with members nurtured in distinctive ways. Professional tribes choose their own leaders and establish their own pecking orders. They impose sanctions on any member of the tribe who does not conform. They expel members who begin to demonstrate the characteristics of another tribe.

In demanding that professionals work in multi-professional teams, we are expecting them to confront, articulate and lay to one side the distinctiveness of their long-established 'tribal' beliefs and behaviours. It may seem that we are asking them to equate the high status and prestige associated with some professions working within children's services – for example, being a doctor or a speech therapist – with the lower status of others, for example, being a nursery nurse or a health visitor. These constructs of status are associated with gender stereotypes of the professionals delivering children's services – what is seen as appropriate work for men and women. In turn, the constructs have been influenced by the cultural aspirations of boys and girls implicit in their choice of careers – and on their beliefs about how much responsibility they should take and how much they deserve to be paid. Loxley (1997) points out that cultural conflict is interwoven with inter-professional collaboration because of the deep-seated social differences in the division of labour that have developed over the past 200 years in the health and welfare services in the UK.

Hudson (2002) argues that there are three potential barriers to multi-professional working:

- *professional identity*: how professionals understand themselves and their roles;
- *professional status*: how professional hierarchies and different distribution of powers are generated;
- *professional discretion and accountability*: how professionals exercise discretion on a day-to-day basis.

We were able to identify many of these conflicts, tensions and barriers underpinning the daily workplace activities of the teams and in the discourse of the professionals we interviewed. We will explore the evidence in relation to three aspects of professional identity or 'who I am' in multi-professional teamwork: what I bring from my history as a professional; who I am now; and who I am within the team.

We asked each of the professionals we interviewed to describe to us the strengths they brought to their team from the history of their previous, usually single-agency, work experiences. Typical responses were as follows:

> I've done child protection work, as well as work with adults with learning difficulties and before that a long time ago – 20 years ago – I worked as a residential social worker with adolescents, and I've also worked as a community health worker.

> Most of it is an education background, and then seven years of working in a child development assessment unit.

It seemed important to some interviewees who had opted to work in a multi-professional team that they had a flexible approach to work in general. For example, one interviewee explained: 'I think because I did quite a lot of agency work beforehand and I'm used to coming into teams and sort of doing my bit and then moving on and moving around, I'm quite used to it … I've not been like a social worker or nurse who's had a set field for so long and then have to come and redefine it.' This is significant for our study because in many ways the professionals in our teams were 'early adopters' and enthusiasts for a model which may later generate 'conscripts' rather than volunteers.

Another respondent argued that professionals need to be confident enough in their professional identity to let go of previous affiliations: 'People [in our team] don't seem to feel as though their identity is just totally wrapped up with where they've come from, with their professional background. I think that [attitude] harnesses the strengths rather than identifies the weaknesses.' It was also important for professionals that individual professional identities, related to their specialisms, were acknowledged and retained within team functions: 'we have our specialities or personal interests that we bring to the team'.

The period of transformation as newly appointed professionals settled into multi-professional teamwork could be traumatic. Sometimes their sense of who they were as professionals was destabilized. They could be distressed that others were taking on roles and responsibilities that they perceived were traditionally theirs. For example, a nurse told us 'sometimes I have to reflect on other members of the team taking on things that I might have found to be my role'. Teachers found themselves handing over aspects of their work to teaching assistants or learning mentors. Speech therapists were asked to train education staff to deliver treatments to children with language problems, now routinely integrated into mainstream schooling, for whom they would in the past have offered specialized one-to-one treatments in clinics.

One recurring concern of the professionals as they made the transition to a new professional identity was the label they were given. Their concerns were partly to do with how the label influenced perceptions of the world outside the team. As we argued earlier in this chapter, our identity is developed primarily in relation to how others perceive us. For example, one respondent said:

> First of all we called ourselves project workers, which I absolutely hated, because that says we could be someone who had been employed as a volunteer you know, off the streets, without qualifications ... Now we've got this new ghastly term and I can never say it without stumbling over it and people never know what on earth that is.

Others were concerned with how the label affected the perceptions of clients. Two examples emerged from our respondents as follows: 'I feel unhappy with the label but I'm not sure that the community fully understands the label. I think it can be a little confusing' and 'but most people assume because my role is a nursery nurse that I work in a school'. Sometimes the lack of clear labels could cause anxiety to clients receiving treatments: 'I have had families, say, if I've done a few sessions, and they feel the problem is not going away instantly, they will sometimes say "Perhaps we should see a proper psychologist?"' Here questions of status and perception emerge, indicating that language and titles matter in the process of negotiating identity in multi-professional teams.

Other professionals were left adrift with ambivalent labels. This is demonstrated by the following two responses: 'Well, I can't call myself a family therapist because that means something different. It's a very specific thing. I don't know. I'm not sure. But I suppose I say I work with children and families. You know, that's how I'd put it.' And further:

> I suppose there have been a couple of incidents outside work where people have said, 'Oh, what job are you doing now?' and I suppose I have said health visitor because I am not quite ... it is not clear what. So I do feel a lack of clarity really about my professional role. Because although I am actually

a seconded health visitor, so I was very clear about that, now that I am a mental health practitioner I am not as clear.

Here we get a profound feel of the dilemmas posed by shifting and changing professional identities. This is a core experience of professionals practising in multi-professional teams.

A second concern was how colleagues within the team perceived them. In well-established teams there was clarity that individuals were expected to adopt a new, 'corporate' identity. So, for example, a team member told us: 'I would be worried if I heard a colleague saying "Hello, I'm a social worker in the child development team." I would think, no you're not, you're a child development team worker who used to be a social worker.'

In another team a professional explained that adopting a new professional identity involved jettisoning past identities: 'I see myself, professional identity, as a CAMH worker, that's how I see myself. I don't see myself as an ex-teacher or a counsellor. I see myself as a CAMH worker.'

Professionals who were core to teams seemed better able to cope with identity transformations. So, for example, a core member of the child development team confidently reported: 'I think myself and the physio do a lot of role blurring together in terms of treating the child as a whole in certain aspects, but I don't feel threatened by that. I know some people probably might.' Those who worked in the team part-time or for short-term secondments, or who perhaps perceived their work to be less valued, seemed to find it harder. For example: 'You know, I have been a nurse and a health visitor for a lot of years and taught suddenly to stop being one. And there are certain situations I have been in with clients where I may be aware that the focus of my work is being driven by my background.'

There is a key issue here about differences between what we might identify as 'core' and 'peripheral' team members – an issue that we return to later.

There was also a related issue about how status affected one's professional identity. Though there was general recognition that the status of a profession had an impact on one's professional identity, a social worker reported: 'I am not overawed by working with people just because they have got a tall hat on, but a lot of people are, and I think a lot of people with tall hats are overawed by their own status as well. Sometimes people aren't listening to each other.'

More positively, there was acknowledgement that working in multi-professional teams eroded traditional constructs of power/status by demystifying what others do: 'It's broken down a few barriers, working with paediatricians. They're just like another profession to me. I don't feel the need to put them on a pedestal. They're down to earth like everyone else on the team. It's having the knowledge of the work they do and working alongside them.'

Peripheral or isolated team members had to work hard to get their voices heard. One professional said, 'Sometimes it feels undermining to say, "Well, only our way is valuable", when from my point of view I have to say, well, this is valuable and that is valuable, but sometimes it seems that is not taken on board.' Sometimes being heard was about a person's personality rather than their status or identity within a team: 'I think that because it's very rare that I have opinions, because I am usually quite quiet, but at least when I have an opinion, it is acknowledged.'

Those professionals who were able to weather the storms of identity transformation emerged with new confidence and self-awareness:

> It's made me think much, much more about the way in which I communicate my identity to others and with others. In terms of my identity, it's made me think about what I don't do and what I can't do as much as what I can do. And that's difficult because that often involves saying to people no, and that often involves saying to people yes.

Professionals, then, can emerge from challenges to their identity with a new and positive sense of their professional self.

A number of themes about the implications of working in a multi-agency team emerged for 'who I am':

- professionals need to be confident enough about the professional identity they bring to multi-professional teams to feel safe about transforming it;
- in the period of adjusting to their new roles and assuming different identities in multi-professional teamwork, professionals may feel anxious, destabilized and vulnerable;
- those who are peripheral to core team membership, or feel isolated as lone representatives of a profession in a team are likely to feel less well supported in transitions to new identities;
- professionals believed that the labels assumed by or imposed on them had an impact on how they were perceived both within and outside the team;
- the perceived status of professionals in the world beyond the team did impact on team functions, but these barriers could be broken down over time;
- professionals who struggled through the pain of transformation to the gains of a new professional identity reported an enhanced sense of 'who I am'.

Conclusion

This chapter focused on how professionals cope with changing roles and responsibilities when working in multi-professional teams and how these changes impact on their professional identities. In the next chapter we turn to the vexed question of how professionals deal with sharing their professional knowledge and transferring their skills to other team members within the daily working activities of multi-professional teamwork.

Think points

- How would you describe your professional identity?
- Has this changed in recent years?
- If you work in a multi-disciplinary setting, is there a shared identity? Or do people hold on to their original professional identity? What impact does this have on the way you work?

6

Sharing knowledge in the multi-professional workplace

Mark Robinson, Angela Anning and Nick Frost

In this chapter we explore how professionals working in integrated children's services share knowledge and expertise within their teams. In other words, the focus is on 'what I know' and 'what I am able to do' in daily work-based activities as a member of a multi-professional team.

The nature of professional knowledge

There has always been a tension in the workplace in reconciling the propositional knowledge of professionals, often acquired in training for qualifications, with the application of that knowledge to the 'real world' of the workplace. Applied knowledge is initially learned as professionals work alongside experienced workers, either on placements during their initial training (e.g. nurses attached to hospital wards or teachers to schools) or in induction periods at the start of their careers (e.g. the probationary year for teachers in schools or the close supervision of therapists in their first years at work). Lave and Wenger (1991) call this apprenticeship style of work-based learning 'legitimate peripheral participation'.

Much professional knowledge remains tacit in the workplace, expressed only by implication in what professionals actually do: how a teacher structures a learning activity, how a speech therapist diagnoses speech delay, how a health visitor weighs a baby. Professionals, particularly those regarded as of lower status, have rarely been required to articulate their knowledge in action to anyone else. It may be that practitioners' only experience of explaining their working practices to an audience has been in encounters with trainees. This may have been a comfortable experience of a student 'learning by Nelly', where the trainee was in the dependent and the practitioner was in the dominant mode of learning. In contrast, in multi-professional teamwork settings, professionals are expected to explain their knowledge, and demonstrate their expertise, to a wide range of other professionals with different status, work experiences and qualifications. This may be a much less comfortable experience for a practitioner. Colleagues in teams may ask challenging questions about the assumptions underpinning their work. They really do want to understand what other team members know and do.

Michael Eraut draws a distinction between two types of professional knowledge. He defines 'C' or codified knowledge 'in terms of propositional knowledge, codified and stored in publications, libraries and databases and so on ... and given foundational status by incorporation into examinations and qualifications' (1999: 3). He defines 'P' or personal knowledge 'in terms of what people bring to practical situations that enables them to think and perform. Such personal knowledge is not only acquired through the use of public knowledge, but also constructed from personal experience and reflection.'

When practitioners are asked to talk about their knowledge and skills in the workplace, they are more likely to refer to the P kind of knowledge acquired from their daily workplace experiences. They are less likely to refer to the theoretical underpinnings implicit in their activities at work. Yet this is the C kind of knowledge which formed the basis of their training to be, for example, a doctor, social worker or teacher. Though practitioners rarely articulate it, they do in fact have 'theories' underpinning their practice. For example, the professionals in the five multi-professional MATCh project teams referred to theories in Chapter 4 when we discussed the constructs of childhood and treatments they espoused.

Theories are built up over years of practice as individual professionals plan strategies for treatments, encounter recurring kinds of problems, deploy particular kinds of activities and reflect on whether treatments do or do not work. Their theories are refined when familiar, expected responses from their clients do not happen. When these unexpected responses occur, professionals have to take stock, rethink their plans and try new approaches to treating clients. As they reflect on what they have learned from meeting the challenges of this particular novel case, they accommodate new insights into their ever-expanding general theories about their work. A similar process will happen following organizational or policy change when professionals confront new and initially unfamiliar problems. As we will discuss later in this chapter, this expansive learning can be strengthened when such individual insights are shared across professional teams, rather than held within just one individual professional's expanding knowledge base.

Professionals on vocational courses either at pre- or post-qualification need to be trained in both propositional (C) and experiential (P) knowledge. C knowledge is more susceptible to being assessed by written examinations and tests, while P knowledge is more likely to be assessed through competence-based models such as portfolios, observations of practitioners at work or oral examinations. These related but different forms of assessment tend to affect the status of knowledge acquired. For example, a degree assessed by written exams tends to be valued more highly than a diploma assessed by portfolios of competence. Moreover, professionals undergoing initial training tend to be trained in very specific P knowledge disciplines and related C knowledge vocational practices. This has implications for the way in which specialist knowledge and expertise are deployed, valued and paid for in the systems and structures of the workplace.

Researchers and commentators have identified the distinct agendas of professional training domains as militating against joined-up working. For example, Petrioni (1994: 84) wrote: 'The concept of inter-professional collaboration is not something that any of the professions were, or to a great extent are, trained for. Indeed they may be receiving training which specifically educates against inter-professional work. Research amongst health and social care students seems to support this view.'

The policy shift towards multi-professional work has promoted a radical rethinking of the training of professionals to work in children's services, both at pre-service and in-service phases. We will return to the broader issues of workforce reform in later chapters when we discuss the practical implications of research into joined-up thinking and working.

How knowledge and expertise are shared in multi-professional teams

Conventional models of adult and child learning emphasize the individual, private ownership of knowledge and skills. The shift towards integrated service delivery has highlighted the importance of knowledge distributed across groups of people through both formal and informal mechanisms. This concept of 'distributed knowledge' is at the heart of new ways of thinking about learning. It challenges the conventions of developmental psychology with its emphasis on the attainments of individual learners. As Puonti (2004: 44) argues: 'The human mind is distributed among people, their representations and artefacts. Knowledge, is not merely "in the head", it is also "in the world" and "between people".' Such radical new concepts demand new ways of researching them. Researchers are developing new ways of observing learning which do not rely as heavily as in the past on assessing individuals' learning through language, or observing it through performances on (sometimes laboratory-based) practical tests.

Another important construct is that if knowledge is distributed across a group of workers in a multi-professional team, the knowledge will be dictated by the nature of the teamwork, its location and history. Each individual professional also brings to the team their own histories, knowledge and skills. So the combined knowledge base of teams is inevitably fluid as well as situated in a particular sociocultural-historical context. As policy and practice shift, the knowledge base changes in response to new demands on the systems and structures of the team as an entity. But it also changes as individuals join or leave the team. In consequence, there can be no ideal model of an appropriate knowledge base for multi-professional teamwork. Rather, joined-up working can be seen as a fluctuating, local, working context and fluid set of practices where knowing and learning are characterized by tensions and conflicting beliefs.

Sorting out structural aspects of teamwork is important, but acknowledging the complexity of the processes by which the team learns new ways of working together is of equal importance. These complexities are often lost in taken-for-granted assumptions about improving the 'efficiency' of multi-professional team-work by enforcing structural changes. Such bland assumptions do not address the 'effectiveness' of multi-professional teamwork by acknowledging the nuances of the evidence of how professionals learn to work in new ways and the centrality of informal learning. In this book we try to give equal attention to understanding and managing both the structural and process aspects of change.

Informal exchanges of knowledge

We asked members of the five multi-professional teams in the MATCh project how they shared and redistributed knowledge and expertise. They told us about the informal and formal ways this happened. The informal ways could be chats in corridors or gossiping as they stood around photocopiers: 'I think just chatting in a team room or over lunch or whatever ... we've been very open in sharing our skills with each other anyway.'

Sometimes informal exchanges were to do with a particular client's needs. A social worker in the youth crime team explained: 'You get a young person coming through the system and you want to go and chat to someone about him or her and say "I've got this person and what do you think?" And they might know them.'

It was relatively easy to draw on the youth crime team's network of general and specific knowledge among their probation officers, learning mentors, police officers and health workers, because they all worked in the same building. In jargon terms they were 'co-located'. Even so, part-timers who came into the team offices at certain times each week could feel peripheral to these transient networks of local knowledge passed casually between colleagues in informal exchanges.

Another important feature of the teams' informal ways of working was through social events set up with the purpose of getting to know each other and offering mutual support. Wenger argued that 'in order to be a full participant [of a community of practice] it may be just as important to know and understand the latest gossip as it is to know and understand the latest memo' (1998: 74). For teams in the MATCh project, knowledge of each other at an interpersonal level was seen to be as important as knowledge of each other as professionals in order for the team to function effectively. A member of the youth crime team explained: 'We go out maybe once every couple of months, but that's a whole team group. But in between times, like if someone's stressed or something, then we'll go to the pub for lunch.' Other teams had regular sandwich lunches together, or provided cakes to enliven team meetings on the weeks when it was someone's birthday. The interpersonal aspects of getting to know about each other established trust, so that when the going got rough in meetings, the team could fall back on relationships they had forged over time to help get through the pain of conflicts to the gain of resolutions.

Team members frequently mentioned the importance of retaining a sense of humour, particularly when stress levels were high. Typical comments were: 'We have a lot of shared humour and a lot of respect for each other and for different things, and that has been part of the success of the team'; 'Most of us have a pretty good sense of fun and I think that's important, and a lot of caring for each other'; 'I think we're quite well able to talk to each other and challenge each other and tease each other'. Humour plays an important part in helping to build and sustain the multi-professional team.

Formal exchanges of knowledge: meetings

Formal ways of exchanging knowledge were based on prearranged team meetings or training events. All the five teams valued regular team meetings as a forum for the exchange of knowledge and expertise. Some of the teams had established strategies of one kind or another to divide the business of team meetings into two halves. One half was devoted to 'business stuff', for example, reporting and disseminating information about new national or local authority policies/regulations. The other half was allocated to aspects of team functioning. For example, the young people's team 'found team meetings were becoming exhausting and we agreed, look, let's do a business part first and anything we need to reflect on and sort out and argue about is given a separate slot'. They took a break between the two halves of the agenda to share a coffee and chat informally before tackling the 'difficult' part of the meeting. The child development team arranged monthly meetings with three short meetings to discuss the pragmatics of cases and a longer one timetabled each month to focus on shared learning activities: 'So, for instance, this Friday we are looking at report-writing and in June I am doing a presentation to the team on aspects of the research I've been looking at.' Those on part-time contracts often found it difficult to attend team meetings. This increased their sense of exclusion from the processes of developing a distributed knowledge base. They could also feel dislocated from a shared understanding of agreed practices in their team.

Formal exchanges of knowledge: training/learning together

Training events could be add-ons to the team meetings. For example, the youth crime team invited experts to give presentations at their regular team meetings to update them on aspects of policy and practice where they perceived they had gaps. When team members were released to attend training events relevant to the team's functioning, they were expected to feed back what they had learned to their colleagues at the next team meeting. Other training events were one-off sessions or away days. Away days were often designed to address substantial shifts in aspects of team responsibilities and ways of working. Sometimes these expensive away days could be subverted into exploring ways of responding to central directives from the government. So a youth justice worker told us: 'I would like to see some time going back to team away days that looks at other things than just targets. Looks at relationships in the team, the fluidity, who is making decisions, who is connecting with who well, where are the developmental links that need to be worked at?'

The young people's team organized regular group supervision/seminar sessions led by different team members to disseminate their specialist knowledge and expertise among the team: 'Different people will lead depending on what we've agreed to look at. So we've looked at families that have step-parents ... reconstituted families ... and there's a huge amount of professional reflection and learning in those groups.'

Sometimes the training emerged from colleagues working together on joint activities. For example, in the child development team, the psychologist told us:

> If you do it together, you get it together. And so actually going on home visits and doing things in people's front rooms with colleagues is what really binds the system. Because you're actually trusting each other and you're seeing each other doing it. You're not doing it separately. And you're not reading bits of paper. You actually experience the other person working with the child, or the parent, and I've got a lot out of that.

The child development team held joint assessments of the children when the whole team and the parents were present. The assessments were done by two of the professionals working with the children and parents, with the rest of the team observing through a one-way mirror. They each took turns in doing the assessments. The team used the sessions both to confer on possible diagnoses and treatments of the specific case they had observed, but also to develop a shared general knowledge base of assessing, diagnosing and deciding on treatments for their client group: 'We take turns in going to observe a child, then we give formal feedback, from what we found, to each other. And then we go back and give that feedback verbally to the parents. After that we come back together and talk about the assessment and how we have given the feedback.' This way of working requires a high degree of trust between team members. The professionals in this team told us:

> We're all interdependent ... because people all have their own roles to play and they're playing them together, that makes a team operate as a team ... And we've got that shared role, that shared interest which is the assessment of the child and the focus on the child and family needs.

The team had experimented with videotaping some of the sessions to enable more reflection on the details of the evidence and decisions about treatments.

Again, such an approach presupposes a well-developed climate of trust within a team and a robust code of ethics. Research in the field shows us that the temptation with video evidence of the realities of professional practice is to focus on the minutiae of negative aspects of practice before panning back to discuss the more global, positive aspects of the events recorded. Again, we noted how important humour was in coping with this degree of exposure of professional selves to others: 'We've started videoing our assessments and looking at how we do it ... sit down and look at ourselves, and have a good laugh as well as seeing how it operates. And I think we've had the confidence to do that together, and it's been okay.'

Another kind of joint activity was when consultants observed physiotherapists and occupational therapists working together on the wards with children so that they could see for themselves what the problems might be with a particular child they were treating. When they had regular team meetings, these shared experiences and observations of the child provided 'the unified front of this is what we think' about a case. In the youth crime team, regular case discussions gave professionals the opportunity to bring different perspectives on how they might approach working with a young person 'when everything seems to be so stuck'.

Professionals also pooled their knowledge and expertise as a team to train others to work with young people. For example, 'a newer member of our team has just done a consultation with learning mentors on eating disorders, and also we did an earlier one on depression. So she has had the chance to co-teach with me, and indeed me with her, and we've learnt from each other perhaps additional skills in presenting together'. Finally, a key worker might take the role of advocate at team meetings for a particular child, pulling together information about him or her for everyone else to share. In one case the nurse at the youth crime team did an audit of the health needs of young people in general by consulting with groups of them. She then became the advocate for a client group, rather than an individual client, feeding the knowledge she had gained back to the team.

Consensus and conflict as the catalyst for learning

As we have seen, the notion of a community of practice as a place where members of the community learn from each other is a recurring theme in Wenger's model (Lave and Wenger 1991; Wenger 1998). Community members work to achieve a cultural consensus and a shared discourse about their daily work experiences. For Wenger, the association of community and practice involves three elements: joint enterprise, mutual engagement and a shared repertoire. Defining a joint enterprise is not about a 'static agreement' between members of the community, but is likely to be 'a process'. Mutual engagement brings to the members relations of mutual accountability. A shared repertoire is characterized by participation in joint activities, and their reification into objects which are external manifestations of their ways of working together. Reification might be record-keeping systems, office equipment, shared discourse and tools. Some of these reifications become 'boundary objects' designed to exemplify new ways of working at the cutting edge of emerging new practices. An example is the Common Assessment Framework to which a range of professionals and a child's parents contribute in order to focus on a case. Boundary objects can form the bridge between traditional inherited ways of working, which have been brought to the community of practice by various constituencies coming together to forge the new community.

Wenger argues that communities of practice are not necessarily harmonious and cooperative, but essentially his model is about working steadily towards agreement and stability in work-based learning. Engestrom et al. (1999: 345) take a rather different starting point. For them, interagency collaboration 'requires active construction of constantly changing combinations of people and artefacts over lengthy trajectories of time and widely distributed in space'. In the modern world of work, practice is characterized by what they call 'knot working'. They argue that teamwork is best conceived not as focusing on particular actors. Instead, it is a combination of situation-specific, object-orientated, distributed activities. As they argue, 'The unstable knot itself needs to be made the focus of analysis' (Engestrom et al. 1999: 347).

Engestrom argued that the best way to study and understand these knots is to investigate them in boundary-crossing laboratories set up in the workplace for that purpose. His techniques, involving, for example, videotaping critical incidents and replaying them to those involved, are designed to get workers to bring to the surface contradictions between their previous histories of ways of working and proposed new ways of working within their teams. Thus the recognition and articulation of conflicts are seen as an essential element in managing change. His work has been particularly focused on health settings (e.g. Engestrom 2000) where he has used videotapes of encounters between professionals and patients as the basis for dialogue about different perspectives on diagnoses and treatments.

Another important construct in Engestrom's (2001) work is that of expansive learning. He argues that learning in work organizations is too complex to be understood within standard theories of learning 'where a subject (traditionally an individual, more recently possibly an organization) acquires some identifiable knowledge or skills in such a way that a corresponding, relatively lasting change in the behaviour of the subject may be observed'. Essentially, learning is traditionally understood as a vertical process, with learners progressing upward to higher levels of competence. Instead he argues that:

> People and organizations are all the time learning something that is not stable, not even defined or understood ahead of time. In important transformations of our personal lives and organizational practices, we must learn new forms of activity which are not yet there. They are literally learned as they are being created.

(2001: 137)

Engestrom argues that we need a complementary perspective on knowledge creation, premised on horizontal, expansive learning and development. He believes
that both service providers and clients should be involved in cycles of reflection
on evidence of real episodes in the workplace. Professionals are then prompted
to use insights gained from their expansive learning to initiate new activities. In
turn, reflection on these activities enables them to enter a new cycle of expanding their understanding and refining their practice.

Another important area of research and debate is how we reconcile the specialisms professionals bring to teams with the requirement for a team to operate
in a holistic, general way. Atkinson et al. (2001) found that interagency working promotes the development of hybrid professional types, 'who have personal
experience and knowledge of other agencies, including importantly, these services' cultures, structures, discourses and priorities'. One stumbling block is the
distinct discourses or language of professionals which may exclude others from
some aspects of team discussions and decision-making. But professionals can
and do learn the skills of being able to communicate with each other about their
specialist knowledge and skills.

Yet specialisms need to be recognized and respected within a team. It is
important that they are deployed strategically for the maximum benefits of
service users and most economic ways of deploying the skills of a multiprofes-
sional workforce. As the team for the ESRC Teaching and Learning Research
Programme III (Warmington et al. 2004) argued, we should be able to recognize the key role of specialist knowledge within multi-professional teams, while
promoting opportunities for relevant aspects of that knowledge to be distributed within the teams. Warmington et al. cite Granville and Langton as follows
(2004: 24):

> There has been an ongoing tension between specialism and generalism.
> They [practitioners of different disciplines] have needed to maintain and
> value the distinct skills and knowledge that particular disciplines offer. There
> is, however, an overall recognition of the considerable gains to be derived
> from the pragmatic necessity of a more integrated way of working.

If professionals feel that their distinctive knowledge base and skills remain valued while they are open to expanding their learning to enrich them, they are
more likely to feel comfortable about their professional identity and gain greater
job satisfaction. They can also feel reassured that their career trajectories as
specialists remain intact beyond the life of the multi-disciplinary team.

Conclusion

A number of themes have emerged from the focus of this chapter on 'what I
know' and 'what I am able to do' in working in multi-professional teams:

- much knowledge in the workplace remains tacit, but professionals working in multi-agency teams are required to make it explicit for their colleagues;
- there are two types of knowledge – codified and personal – and professionals need to be trained to deploy both in the workplace;
- professionals generate theories about their work through daily situated experiences of and reflection on delivering services;
- multi-professional teamwork offers opportunities for professional knowledge and expertise of individuals to be distributed across the team;
- the team carries the sociocultural histories both of individual workers and of the institution, and all this changes as the nature of work and team membership fluctuates;
- knowledge and expertise are shared in informal exchanges in the workplace and social events;
- knowledge and expertise are shared in the formal planned contexts of meetings and training events, and in joint activities between professionals in the workplace;
- there may be a tension between the desire to reach consensus (as in a community of practice model) and to confront conflict (as in a knot working model);
- service providers and users can learn from each other in cycles of expansive learning to deepen their understanding of and refine workplace activities;
- it is important to respect and deploy distinctive specialisms, as well as general understanding, if professionals are to gain job satisfaction and retain opportunities for career advancement beyond the life of the multi-professional team in which they currently work.

In Part 3 of the book we focus on putting some of our findings into practice and explore some key practice issues in two chapters exploring how to implement the MATCh findings. The following four chapters (9–12) in Part 4 explore the application of multi-professional working in the four specific fields:

- leadership and the organization of initial assessment teams;
- information-sharing;
- special educational needs and disability;
- child sexual exploitation.

In the final chapter of the book we will focus on lessons learned from research and scholarship for the practicalities of making multi-professional teamwork work.

Think points

- How does learning get shared in your workplace or placement?
- Make a list of informal ways of sharing learning.
- Make a list of formal ways of sharing learning.
- Make three suggestions to improve the sharing of professional knowledge in your workplace/placement.

Part 3

Planning, implementing and supporting multi-professional teams working with children

In this part of the book we suggest how our MATCh findings can be utilized to influence policy and practice in relation to multi-professional work with children and their families.

7

Making it work 1 – addressing key dilemmas

Angela Anning and Nick Frost

Introduction

In this chapter we examine two aspects of making multi-professional teamwork successful. In the first part of the chapter we use the evidence we gained from discussing key incidents in the daily working lives of our sample of professionals engaged in delivering integrated services. In the second half of the chapter we extend the discussion to dilemmas common to multi-professional teams and suggest some ways they address them. The chapter enables the reader to reflect on some of the real challenges that are embedded within the integrated working agenda.

Addressing some specific incidents in multi-professional teamwork

A powerful tool for encouraging professionals to talk about their work is to encourage them to discuss specific incidents they have encountered. Discussion of specific events often leads to generalizing key principles embedded in their work. During the final phase of the project we asked members of the five MATCh teams to record in a diary over a three-month period four or five examples of critical incidents (either positive or negative) inherent in their multi-professional teamwork. We used their diary entries as the basis for designing six generalized vignettes representative of the most common types of incident they had recorded. We used the vignettes as the stimulus for focus group discussions for groups within the five teams.

Details of the vignettes are given in Chapter 2. The themes embedded in the vignettes included:

- sharing while acknowledging the importance of specialist expertise;
- using common protocols and documentation;

- excluding team members from discussions by the use of jargon;
- brokering links with external agencies;
- resolving differences in the values of team members;
- tensions arising from devolving 'specialist' activities to generalist workers.

The vignettes were generalized incidents based loosely on examples reported in the diaries. It was clear that the incidents resonated with our multi-professional teams. Several participants in the focus groups assumed that a fictionalized vignette was drawn directly from their own or a colleague's diary entries.

At the end of the project we held a validation day to disseminate to and get feedback on our findings from all those who had taken part in the project. A consensus emerged among the audience when we shared the vignettes with them. This gave us confidence to interrogate the transcripts of the focus group discussions, and notes taken at the validation day, for general themes emerging from exploration of the specific, work-based incidents and themes embedded in the vignettes.

When we explored the transcripts of conversations from each of the five focus groups, we found that the teams responded quite differently to the incidents. Teams tended to focus on either interpersonal/professional or organizational concerns. For example, the young people's team, with its history and culture of therapeutic work, discussed the incidents in the vignettes from the perspective of listening to each other's contributions. Then they formulated a sequence of problems as individuals, but from which the team gradually moved towards consensus about what they were going to do to solve the main problem. In Vignette 2.6, parents were complaining to a headteacher that learning mentors were not sufficiently trained or skilled to advise them on parenting skills. An extract from the young people's team discussion of this illustrates the process of problem formulation through dialogue towards resolution:

> *First contributor*: But it's going to become an increasing tension or dilemma when we hit an all-time recruitment crisis, you know. More and more people are moving into roles that they are not sufficiently experienced or skilled to do.

> *Second contributor*: And also certain schoolteachers being very, very dismissive about our kind of work, dismissive of certain kids.

> *Third contributor*: Or it may be that the head is right. Maybe it could be that the learning mentors should not be dealing with this level of problem, with children at risk of exclusion, and we may want to go back to the service in terms of reviewing the agreement.

> *Fourth contributor*: And not just that. You would want to know whether it was having any impact on exclusion.

A second extract from the young people's team dialogue is in response to Vignette 2.2. The incident described a paediatrician's anxieties about sharing office space and in particular the impact on the security of medical records:

> *First contributor:* Is this actually confidentiality or about the person's anxiety about their own status?

> *Second contributor:* You would have to be very careful not to come over as a precious practitioner who wants their own desk with their own computer.

> *Third contributor:* And you would have to be very clear that these were only issues that you have around confidentiality and ethics, and they were not about preciousness.

> *First contributor:* As you say, it needs to be clarified. What is a confidential, legal, minimal standard. And what is really about the person's status in the team.

We found that teams with a relatively autonomous approach to their work were more likely to take a problem formulation approach. Other teams with more direction from central or local government imperatives, for example, the youth crime team, were more likely to take a pragmatic, organizational line in their discussions as to how they would tackle the incidents. Their talk focused more on the systems and protocols that helped them sort out or pre-empt a problem. An example is when the youth crime team was discussing Vignette 2.3, an incident where a team member was excluding others from engaging in debates about treatments – and therefore decision-making – through inappropriate use of jargon:

> *First contributor:* I think it's really important for the management or the structure to possess a very clear remit for having that person there in the first place. Just because money's sloshing around, shall we just get this person in to do this?

> *Second contributor:* Could I say that one of the most important things ... we have got rid of this myth that a case should belong to a probation officer, or a social worker and repel all borders. In our team a case belongs to many different people. There's a lot of people involved and their knowledge and so on ... and this person would actually be playing a real role in each case within the team.

> *Third contributor:* Not necessarily the specialists, but anybody who comes on board, part of their training and the getting to know the team is shadowing the other members and finding out: right, that's your niche ... it's all part of getting to know the rest of the team members and what it is they do and don't do.

A further example of the youth crime team's orientation towards pragmatic, organizational solutions to the dilemmas is this extract from a discussion of Vignette 2.5 where a team is confronted by clashes of values among themselves and clashes over their prioritizing of parent over child perspectives in dealing with a lone parent and his 3-year-old child with complex special needs:

First contributor: Eighty-six per cent of the cases we're involved in don't statutorily involve social services. But there are still parenting issues. And I think that's where our team members have achieved well. Because you have to discuss with your colleagues matters of parenting which essentially come from the different values of the team.

Second contributor: We should have much more limited contact with parents. And there would be great use of parenting orders ... the parent who is absent and the parent who is neglectful ... we will be looking at much more closely in the future.

Another difference in their contributions was that the teams varied in the degree to which they were able or prepared to display dissonance to us. In general, a team was more likely to display consensus where there was a non-hierarchical management structure, as in the child development team. Perhaps this reluctance to express dissent openly was because any threat of conflict within a non-hierarchical team could potentially destabilize the hard-won dynamics of their 'democratic' way of working. Or perhaps their particular team history had promoted and achieved consensus about most treatments through previous hard-won debates long rehearsed and forgotten, and to which we had not been witnesses.

It was not just that team cultures promoted a particular approach to tackling the incidents. Individuals within teams contributed to the discussions through their own personal and professional lenses. For example, a medical worker emphasized that in contributing to team discussions about appropriate treatments, 'I would try to present some evidence base to support my view' but was later able to admit ruefully the limitations of taking a strong evidence-based approach to inform all decisions: 'Because you do get that bloody psychologist banging on about the evidence base rather than anything else they could talk about.'

Sometimes the point at which a particular professional lens would be set aside, or not, was related to the potential effect on a client. For example, a clinical psychologist argued:

If they think we should do X and I think we should do Y, what are the consequences of doing X if I think Y is right? Are the consequences terribly adverse for doing X? And how strongly I feel about it would determine what I would do then. If I felt a real serious clinical concern that this kid might top themselves or something terrible, I would really go for it.

The transcripts provided compelling evidence of the importance of acknowledging the sociocultural-historical context in which each version of multi-professional practice is situated and operationalized, rather than assuming a one-size-fits-all approach to their design, implementation and management. The dialogues evidenced the fluidity and flexibility with which teams have to learn to accommodate the views of individual professionals as they come and go within the life of a team. Consequently, we would argue that managing multi-professional teams requires an approach to leadership that maintains a sense of overall direction, while being ready to adapt rapidly to changes in team membership as well as workplace priorities. To be a good manager you have to be a chameleon, responding appropriately to changing circumstances.

Dilemmas common to multi-professional teams

Reflecting on our own research and reports of others engaged in trying to understand the complexities of multi-professional teamwork, we identified recurring dilemmas confronting teams. The dilemmas operated at both team and individual levels. Sometimes individuals confronted personal/professional dilemmas that conflicted with dilemmas for the whole team. In these situations a professional had to decide whether they subjugated their personal, practical dilemmas or inner conflicts in the interest of team maintenance.

Yet we found little evidence of the recognition of the key role emotions were playing in team maintenance in either research reports or theoretical models of multi-professional teamwork. For many professionals who were catapulted into multi-professional teamwork, the emotional aspects of coping with changes in their working lives are underestimated both in the preparation and training offered to them.

The recurring dilemmas are summarized in Tables 7.1 to 7.3. We will discuss each separately before returning to a general discussion of implications of the model for implementing multi-professional teamwork. In the Appendix we provide a checklist that can be utilized by multi-professional teams in developing their teamwork.

Structural dilemmas

Structural dilemmas reported by the teams are summarized in Table 7.1. They include dilemmas for the whole team and for individuals.

The governments of England, Wales, Scotland and Northern Ireland are committed to mainstreaming multi-professional teamwork in delivering children's services, as outlined in The Children Act of 2004. In 2006, the Department for Education and Skills (DfES 2006) identified three models of integrated services:

- a multi-agency panel meeting around the needs of a particular case;
- a multi-agency team, often line managed by a team leader, but retaining supervision and training links with their original agencies;

Table 7.1 Structural dilemmas: coping with systems/management change

Team	Individual
Core and peripheral team membership/responsibilities/status	Full- or part-time/seconded or permanent contract and status
Line management within or without the team	Impact on shared decision-making, time, loyalties and commitment to team
Deployment of workloads/activities	Managing own workloads/time/loyalties/responsibilities
Location of team activities	Status, access, agency within team functioning

- integrated services, usually co-located on one site, where permanent multi-agency teams were appointed to deliver integrated support to children and their families.

Usually each local authority has a director of children's services heading up their Children's Trusts. Trusts are responsible for commissioning services across agencies and sectors leading to integrated service delivery. Whether initiatives are promoted at local, regional or national levels, a key finding from research and evaluations is that in order to be sustainable, they must be underpinned by systemic structural changes within the participating agencies, such as health, education, social work, employment and family support. For example, research in the USA highlighted the importance of organizational climate (the service providers' attitudes to clients nested within a cultural system) for positive service quality and outcomes for children (Glisson and Hemmelgarn 1998).

All over the UK, partnership boards were set up to oversee the management of change towards delivering integrated services (Percy-Smith 2005). The intention was that these partnerships were representative of the vested interests contributing to the work of the multi-professional team, including the private and voluntary sectors. However, partnerships, though a useful concept at an ideological level, may be too loose to be effective in practice. Long-term formal policies and budgetary decisions need to be securely established if services are to be managed and sustained effectively over time. So a key requirement for sustaining systemic, structural change is that representation on Trusts includes senior officers within local or regional authorities. Without their experience, commitment and power at the macro level of local policies, complex decisions about budgets, capital investment and sustainability of services are likely to be fudged.

One aspect of the fudging of decisions is that agencies and sectors are reluctant to commit funding streams long term to the staffing of multi-professional teams brought together for short-term initiatives or flagship projects. This is a particular constraint in the current climate of economic instability. Consequently, staff are often seconded from mainstream funding streams on short-term, often part-time, contracts. Being on a temporary or part-time contract has a profound impact on how committed an individual member of staff feels to their work. Often seconded or part-time staff feel peripheral to the core team structure. Whether a colleague is seconded and/or part-time may also influence the perceptions of core members of the team of their colleague's value to the team's work.

An additional dilemma for seconded or part-time staff may be a lack of clarity about their line management. Sometimes they feel that they have divided loyalties or that their mainstream agency (which pays their salary and has responsibility for their appraisals) is pulling them in a different direction from a manager in the multi-professional team to which they have been 'loaned'. An example would be a teacher who is being asked to reconfigure services to offer informal learning through play opportunities to parents and young children attending family support services, while at the same time being actively encouraged to prepare children to acquire literacy and numeracy skills in a preschool setting by a lead educational partner.

Managers may be uncertain about how best to deploy workloads to professionals within their teams. They have little in the way of an evidence base to help them make decisions. Though we are constantly being reassured that multi-professional teamwork is 'better' for children and their families, much of the evidence to support this claim is anecdotal. For example, it seems obvious that families with children with special needs prefer to have a key worker who collates their case history. There can be nothing more debilitating than to endlessly repeat the same information to a range of agencies contributing to their child's health and well-being. The key worker for a family may be a generic family worker. Yet parents also need the reassurance that sustained, specialist help is deployed strategically when their child needs it. The deployment of specialist expertise and activities at point of need is a challenge for those trying to set up systems for structural change in integrated children's services. Meanwhile, professionals have reported feeling that their specialist expertise, which they know is of benefit to a generation of children, is being frittered away in endless team meetings to rethink workloads, activities and protocols to support the setting up of integrated services systems. This feeling of 'loss' may be exacerbated because often it is practitioners who have been most 'successful' in a single discipline who are seconded into radical, new ways of working in innovative multi-agency teams. They have to start all over again at rebuilding a sense of competence.

Finally, those deployed to work in multi-professional teams are often relocated to new workplaces. For all of us, the environment in which we work is crucial to our sense of well-being. Shifts in furniture, room size, workstations and rest rooms are metaphors for how much we see ourselves as valued people as well as practitioners. In a single agency setting a professional may have worked for years to 'win' a comfortable office and clinic space. For many professionals, a physical move to work in a multi-professional team may result in them losing these hard-won perks. Co-locating can be a debilitating experience. Professionals may have spent years in familiar surroundings in schools, hospitals or family centres. Suddenly their physical workplace looks and feels completely different. The mixed messages of unfamiliar configurations of furniture in integrated service settings – social services-type sofas and coffee tables, mixed with child-sized chairs for pre-school sessions and health-related consulting rooms for clinics – make for uneasiness. Suddenly you do not know where you fit any more. You do not know who you are.

Yet staff told us that it makes a huge difference to a sense of belonging to a team if you are located in the same building as your colleagues. It also makes a difference if you have a workstation which you can personalize in some way. But in transferring to work in a multi-professional team base, you may be expected to work in shared spaces and even at communal workstations. Hot-desking may seem to be an economic imperative to managers dealing with complex staffing and shift patterns of work, but it may not in real terms result in a more effective workforce of highly skilled and autonomous professionals.

Ideological dilemmas

Table 7.2 summarizes the dilemmas associated with ideological similarities and differences within the team.

Table 7.2 Ideological dilemmas: sharing and redistributing knowledge/skills/beliefs

Team	Individual
Dominant models/disciplines/personalities	Accepting/celebrating multi-disciplinarity and diversity
Professional/socio/historical cultures colliding	Having a voice/respect for own professional knowledge and skills
Creating new forms of knowledge	Destabilization of disciplinary habits, beliefs and boundaries

In Chapter 4 we explored the differences and similarities in the constructs of family and childhood held by professionals with different training, values and beliefs. In turn, these constructs determined their understanding of causes and attributions of blame for their clients' situations, social conditions and decisions about preferred treatments or actions. An important example might be when a team brings their different beliefs to addressing the needs of a family where a child's behaviour is disrupting family life and impeding the child's progress at school. A social services approach might be to consider the context in which the whole family has been destabilized. An expert on parenting programmes might argue for parallel strands of behaviour modification for both the parents and their child. An educationalist might argue for raising the child's sense of self as learner and classmate within the context of learning and socializing at school.

The important point is that these different professional voices have a right to be heard within multi-professional teamwork. In fact, the central argument for joined-up working is that the multiple perspectives enrich the treatments offered to clients. As we argued in Chapter 5, for many professionals their knowledge and beliefs have remained implicit in their daily activities and decision-making at work. Suddenly within a multi-professional team they are required to make those beliefs explicit. They are expected to articulate long-held values and defend and justify routine activities. They may only have had to do so in the past when they were involved in training students, in situations when their power was dominant. In the context of working within a multi-professional team they may have to articulate their professional knowledge and justify their professional actions to a group of challenging colleagues. This can be threatening, particularly when their status is not high, for example, when they are a 'junior' member of the team or where they are line managed by a 'high status' manager in their team from a different discipline.

In Chapter 6 we focused on the dilemmas faced by colleagues when their traditional disciplinary beliefs, habits and boundaries were destabilized. We argued that the process of destabilization can make professionals feel disempowered and deskilled. Managers need to be aware of the need to support professionals as they struggle with feelings of disorientation. It takes time for professionals to adjust to broadening their knowledge base and to learn new skills. Yet many professionals attest to the exhilaration of creating new forms of knowledge, both as individuals and within the distributed knowledge base of their teams. Sadly much of this new-found confidence and creativity can be lost as teams are broken up and displaced in response to a series of 'new' government initiatives.

An informative example is provided by the breaking up in 2005–6 of many Sure Start local programme teams, many of which were managed creatively by independent companies or charities, but which were seen to be operating some-what erratically across the country (NESS 2005d), in order to fit them into local authority structures and systems for the launch of Children's Centres. As one manager said, 'It's like turning a huge ship around. We're like the small tug in the middle of huge waves. And I can't get my small boat on course' (NESS 2004: 3).

Procedural dilemmas

Table 7.3 summarizes the dilemmas reported by teams in the day-to-day procedural aspects of their work.

It is one thing to think and talk about delivering children's services in multi-professional teams, but quite another to actually do so on a day-to-day basis. As previously mentioned, the model we used to try to conceptualize the complexities of the procedures of daily service delivery was Wenger's (1998) community of practice at work, in which complementary processes are *participation*

Table 7.3 Procedural dilemmas: participation and reification in delivering services

Team	Individual
Creating common protocols/procedures/documentation	Adjusting to other agency imperatives/issues to do with confidentiality and information-sharing
Deployment of specialists and generalists at user interface	Concerns about status/time/competence
Confronting disagreements about treatments and interventions	Holding onto/letting go of strongly held beliefs and practices
Achieving targets/goals set by local/national imperatives	Coping with pace of change/risks/uncertainties/alienation in activities

(the daily, situated actions and shared experiences of members of the team working towards common goals) and *reification* (the explication of versions of knowledge into representations in the working day such as documentation, dialogue or artefacts).

For both individual professionals and teams a particular challenge is in creating the reification of common protocols, procedures and documentation. A recurring, practical problem is that many single-agency records and procedures are in a state of flux as information storage and retrieval systems are continually being redesigned to accommodate new government and management directives. Sometimes changes in record-keeping systems are linked to agencies being required to demonstrate that they are meeting new government targets. Databases may be completed unevenly, often because staff are not rigorously trained in how to input data correctly, in different institutional settings. Software systems may be unable to deal with an ever-increasing volume of information.

A second major dilemma is that of confidentiality. Social services staff may be concerned that confidential information, particularly in child protection cases, may be released to 'inappropriate' personnel. Medical staff are equally cautious about sharing data on individual or family health. Yet government policy, enshrined in *Working Together to Safeguard Children* (DfE 2015), is that information-sharing should not to be a barrier, in particular in relation to safeguarding children and young people.

The evidence on the ground is that developing common systems and related documentation for identifying, diagnosing and delivering children's services is developing rapidly – particularly in relation to the development of MASHs.

Another major preoccupation in the workplace is how best to deploy specialists (such as midwives and social workers) and generalists (such as peer mentors for promoting breastfeeding, and family support workers). In the field of medicine, where traditionally roles have been more hierarchical, systems of tiers of assessment, diagnosis and treatment have long been established. In Chapter 3 we gave an example of how this works when we described the structure of the two health-based teams in the MATCh project. But in integrated services the role of health visitors in monitoring child health may become blurred with their role in promoting better parenting. Volunteers may be trained to work alongside occupational therapists and play workers in promoting child development. Support workers may be expected to move out of a 'comfort zone' as more activities are devolved to them and they are expected to take on more responsibility. In all this restructuring of systems and redeployment of roles and responsibilities, professionals may lose a sense of satisfaction in their job. For example, a nurse in the youth crime team resented being redefined as a 'jack of all trades'. Professionals may worry about how 'time out' on secondments from their mainstream work will affect their career trajectories. They may be concerned that they are missing crucial training to keep them up to date on professional developments within their own discipline. A speech therapist confessed that this was a real concern to her, despite acknowledging how much she had learned from her extended role in a multi-professional team.

As roles and responsibilities are realigned, questions arise as to who is competent and/or qualified to do what. Who is ultimately responsible for the quality and outcomes of services? Who takes the criticism when an inspection identifies faults in a service or when targets are not met? Is it the head of the employing agency? Or the manager of the multi-professional team to which the employees have been seconded?

Inter-professional dilemmas

Table 7.4 summarizes inter-professional dilemmas in managing the transition to multi-professional teamwork. Different pay and conditions of service are inherited from mainstream agencies. Changes in roles and responsibilities are often initiated without first clarifying how practitioners will reconcile these with their customary hours of working, holiday entitlements and pay structures. Resentments simmer as 'generic' workers perceive that there are inequities in pay, conditions and career trajectories within their teams. An example would be where

Table 7.4 Inter-professional dilemmas: learning through role changes

Team	Individual
Deployments of specialists and generalists	Threats to professional identity/ status and agency
Concerns about competence and supervision	'Comfort' zone and job satisfaction
Training/continuing professional development opportunities for team capacity building	Pay, conditions, career trajectories

teachers working in integrated day care and preschool education settings are on higher salaries than their managers, and yet retain their traditional 'teaching day' working hours and school holiday entitlements. In integrated services for delivering early education and childcare, local authorities are battling to formulate a common funding formula for private daycare settings, voluntary sector preschool playgroups and maintained schools. The intention is to enable the current mixture of private, voluntary and maintained sectors to be sustainable. Workforce reform and revised pay and conditions of service will inevitably result in some providers being less viable than others. Meanwhile, managers of multi-professional teams are taxed with keeping the lid on disputes over pay and conditions, negotiating with the mainstream agencies for temporary solutions to address resentments in order to maintain team functioning.

Conclusion

In this chapter we have presented examples of the way multi-professional teams situated in different sociocultural contexts and with different organizational cultures respond differently to critical incidents in the workplace. Moreover, we have argued that individual professionals within teams respond to incidents differently, each viewing the incident through a particular professional/personal lens. We argue that there is no one version of multi-professional teamwork. The teams are complex organizations demonstrating particular social-cultural-historical characteristics in particular contexts.

Nevertheless, we recognize that multi-professional teams delivering children's services in the UK (and probably wherever they are being introduced into the workplace) face common dilemmas. The dilemmas operate at whole team and individual team membership levels concurrently. We explored recurring dilemmas under four headings: structural, ideological, procedural and interpersonal. The Appendix provides teams with a tool for assessing their current stage of development and moving forward.

In Chapter 8, we move on to explore strategies for resolving dilemmas, focusing in particular on strategies for making decisions and for delivering services for children and young people.

Think points

Choose a vignette from Chapter 2.

- Use the vignette for discussion in a team meeting or similar setting.
- What did you learn from the discussion of this issue?

8

Making it work 2 – strategies for decision-making and service delivery

Angela Anning and Nick Frost

Introduction

> *There is no single way to go about integrating services for children and their families. Local conditions and opportunities for change vary so much that no-one can say, 'This is where you should start and this is where you'll end up.'*
>
> (Miller and McNicholl 2003: 1)

In this chapter we aim to build on the previous chapter by examining the policy and service delivery issues facing multi-professional teams as they attempt to address the challenges of improving service delivery. Drawing on the findings outlined in Part 2 of this book we now attempt to unpick the implications of these findings for policy-making and service delivery (Frost and Lloyd 2006; Robinson et al. 2008; Frost, 2014a, 2014b).

We argue that making the principles of multi-professional working operate in practice involves addressing the following key themes:

- joint procedural work and inclusive planning systems;
- clear lines of accountability;
- employment conditions/individual career/role recognition;
- leadership vision;
- role clarity and a sense of purpose;
- addressing barriers related to status/hierarchies;
- agreed strategic objectives and shared core aims;
- transparent structures for communication with partner agencies;

- co-location of service deliverers;
- acknowledging peripheral team members;
- acknowledging professional diversity;
- awareness of impact of change on service users;
- joint client-focused activities;
- ongoing support for professional development;
- paying attention to 'specialist' skills retention.

Each of these themes will be examined in turn.

Joint procedural work and inclusive planning systems

Whether joint work is taking place within or between organizations, effective multi-professional teamwork requires shared procedures that have been developed with the participation of all professionals involved. These procedures become the solid representations of joined-up working, what Wenger refers to as 'reification'. However, procedures are simply pieces of paper until they are enacted through practice by the front-line professional staff. In reality, practice is an interactive process through which informed, reflective professionals interpret and enact procedures (see Bradbury et al. 2010).

We have seen exemplars in the data from the MATCh study of how multi-professional teams perform complex interactions with policies from outside and procedures from within the teams. This process takes time, especially when people from differing professional backgrounds are coming together. The development of procedures and policies requires skilful leadership from both within and outside the team.

The process of professional participation cannot be seen as static. In the real world, change occurs rapidly with new laws, regulations and changing social factors having a continuous impact on front-line practice. All of the sample teams experienced change during the 18 months of our fieldwork – including one whose role and function changed totally. This is not an unusual experience in the modern workplace (see Castells 1998). As a result of the rapid pace of change, procedures and protocols must be regularly reviewed and consulted about, and when necessary changed and reformed to reflect changes in practice. This process forms part of a learning loop where policy structures practice, but where practice should, in turn, inform and reform policy. Acknowledging the complexity of this interplay of policy and practice has informed the way we have written this book.

Clear lines of accountability

When professionals work in a traditional vertically managed environment, lines of accountability are usually clear and straightforward. When multi-professional working is developed these lines of accountability can become complex and blurred (Øvretveit 1993; and see our discussion and diagrams in Chapter 3). For example, as we have seen, in some teams a worker might be seconded from an agency that retains responsibility for their service conditions, be line managed by the team manager of the multi-professional team and perhaps receive supervision from a third party. Joined-up, multi-professional teams therefore often have complex lines of accountability.

This inherent complexity should not be seen as a barrier to the effective functioning of multi-professional teams – but it does have to be addressed. The organization of the team and lines of accountability need to be transparent and make sense for the front-line worker. It is also important to ensure that they are offered effective support and supervision, both from within and outside the team structure.

Employment conditions, individual career and role recognition

As we discussed in Chapter 5, staff who are engaged in multi-professional team-work will almost inevitably experience challenges to their sense of professional identity and well-being. Their sense of identity was previously built on their feelings of difference (from other professional groups) and a sense of belonging (to their specific professional group). In a multi-professional environment they are asked to reinvent themselves through a connection with other professionals. They will need time and space to reflect on their new professional identity and will require support from line managers and colleagues in dealing with the desta-bilization of their former professional identities.

Alongside issues of identity, there are likely to be some issues concerning service conditions that must be taken into account. Multi-professional teamwork often means different professionals doing the same work. For example, many staff were expected to utilize Common Assessment Frameworks. Where professionals are on different salary scales and service conditions, they may resent this and may ask why they are not being paid as much as another profession doing the same work. Such concerns have to be shared and openly confronted. In the medium to long term, joint working seems to suggest the logic of joint national and local pay and service conditions.

As we have seen from the examples in this book, some professionals wish to hold on to their identity within a multi-professional setting. Others are willing to transform their identity within a new setting and way of working. Whichever journey staff undertake, they are likely to require support and time for reflection. It should be recalled that our sample are in some senses 'early adopters' of this new mode of working and to a certain extent are 'volunteers' and enthusiasts. As multi-professional teams have become increasingly a dominant form of organization, the staff and co-location are becoming more common, and the staff involved may be more coerced and less enthusiastic. Further studies of the views and experiences of these staff will be required as the rollout of integrated working models continues (Atkinson et al. 2007; Robinson et al. 2008).

Leadership vision

A key variable in implementing effective practice in multi-professional team-work is the leadership offered by senior staff. In the MATCh project teams we observed highly skilled and effective leaders working on the cutting edge of practice development. Effective leadership involves individuals who can work in the ever-changing world of integrated working characterized by the skills involved in networking and boundary-crossing. Such leadership has been identified in a number of studies such as those cited below.

> The most effective YOT [youth offending team] managers appear to have strong entrepreneurial skills, which they use to build good relationships with governing bodies and to broker inter-agency agreements. Effective YOTs give managers freedom and flexibility.
>
> (Audit Commission 2004: 57)

> We identified a number of 'boundary spanning' individuals who operated as entrepreneurs in creating new solutions to public policy problems. They had well-developed skills at mobilising political, financial and technical resources from a range of sources and bringing these to bear on particular needs and issues ... these individuals start from the problem rather than the procedures. They are adept at managing the procedures, but only because this is necessary in order to gain access to resources that will deliver their objective.
>
> (Skelcher et al. 2004: 4)

Our findings also suggest that effective leadership is crucial in providing an environment that values people and celebrates the diversity of different professionals. Team members need to be encouraged to celebrate their differences, and also perceive that they are held together by a shared vision and common sense of purpose (Ancona et al. 2007).

Role clarity and a sense of purpose

One of the challenges of flexible multi-professional ways of working is that roles can become blurred and complex. This is a dynamic process of change and challenge that will have specific features in different situations and can only be fully understood in context. Effective multi-disciplinary working should not imply that people lose clarity about their roles. Just as an effective football team will contain players of different attributes and skills to create a successful team, so should a good multi-professional team. Each worker should have a clear role and a definite sense of that role and how they contribute to the overall purposes of the team.

Addressing barriers related to status/hierarchies

Exhortations to work together and to 'join up' should not wish away the reality of status and hierarchical barriers. Here we are dealing with a complex interplay of change and resistance, of difference and conflict. But when diverse professionals come together, they may well find that the differences are not as great as they imagined. Inevitably, interacting on a day-to-day basis in a co-located setting will break down some professional prejudices and ease the practicalities of communication. Equally, coming together may serve to enhance, entrench or even exaggerate aspects of difference and hierarchy among a group of professionals.

It is also the case that the dominant social divisions – around gender, sexuality, disability and ethnicity – do not magically disappear in multi-professional settings. They will remain influential forces of difference and sometimes lead to the oppression of the least powerful.

During the fieldwork for this project we found evidence to suggest that jargon could be used as an instrument of power in order to exclude staff – in team meetings, for example. Attention should be paid to the importance of clarity in the use of language and it should not be taken for granted that all members understand complex medical terms or acronyms, for example. The chair of meetings should insist that acronyms and specialist terms are explained to all team members.

Agreed strategic objectives and shared core aims

Staff in multi-professional teams need to have a clear sense of shared objectives. The success of the Youth Offending Service, for example, is largely based on their shared statutory purpose of 'reducing the level of youth offending'. They also have a shared assessment framework and staff members are normally co-located, and they have multi-agency forms of governance. As the Audit Commission point out: 'The extent to which a YOT's governing bodies share common objectives is critical to good performance' (2004: 57).

Transparent structures for communication with partner agencies

Most multi-professional teams have to relate to a range of agencies who may fund, second, host or manage the team. Whatever these structures and funding streams, and they are often complex, they need to be clear and transparent to providers and users of the service. For example, youth offending teams have a shared executive body on which all stakeholder bodies are represented, often chaired by the chief executive of the local authority, to ensure that partnership can be delivered from the top.

Information-sharing lies at the heart of the government view of multi-professional teams. Exchange of information across agencies and disciplines is no easy matter. Different professions have different codes of confidentiality and differing attitudes towards the sharing of information. It remains to be seen how these tensions will be resolved at local, regional and national levels. Attempts so far to set up shared databases even within one agency, such as health, have been conspicuously unsuccessful.

Co-location of service deliverers

The idea of co-location has become a reality in many services – with Children's Centres, CAMHS and youth offending teams providing prime examples. There is evidence to suggest that co-location (the sharing of office and other space by professionals) enhances communication, learning and understanding of roles (Frost 2005, 2014a, 2014b). It is important to note that co-location assists, but does not guarantee, effective joint working. Our findings indicated that there can still be problems with communication and shared working activities within co-located settings.

Acknowledging peripheral team members

Our work with the teams suggests that one of the unintended consequences of developing multi-professional teams is that they can generate what we identified as 'core' and 'peripheral' team members. Core members might be those who work full-time, who are high status and to whom the team provides a major element of their daily working practice. Peripheral participants may include part-time workers, those seconded into teams for short periods, those 'hot-desking' or those who feel that they are not central to the main purpose of the joint enterprise. People can also feel peripheral where most of the team are co-located but others are not. In one extreme example from our research, a team member did not realize that she was a member of a particular team until we approached her for an interview!

Supportive and effective managers need to recognize the dangers of staff feeling peripheral and excluded, by valuing them, ensuring they have a clear and defined role to play within the team and by ensuring that effective communication channels are in place.

Acknowledging professional diversity

As we discussed in Chapters 5 and 6, multi-professional teams represent differing professions with diverse roles. While multi-professional working attempts to improve coordination between these groups, it should not attempt to ignore differences. Effective managers need to celebrate and value differences, while building a sense of collective purpose. The issue of professional identity is one of the major issues that needs to be addressed in developing multi-professional working (for further discussion, see Robinson et al. 2005).

Awareness of impact of change on service users

In this book we have focused on the inner workings of multi-professional teams. But effective integrated practice also crucially includes partnerships with service users. Practitioners should be acutely aware of the impact of joined-up practice on service users. Evidence is beginning to emerge that suggests that joined-up practice can have a positive impact on service users (*Children and Society*, Special issue 2009; Easton et al. 2013).

Joint client-focused activities

The most effective joined-up working emerges from actual practice – a strong theme of the work of Wenger. As we described in Chapter 6, the teams had a range of strategies for working together on joint activities. One of the teams worked together on real case assessments, with parents present, each contributing their own specialist knowledge and expertise. After casework they held debriefing sessions, using videotaped evidence, to reflect on how their roles and skills had been deployed. These dialogues provided powerful opportunities for developing a community of practice. Integrated practice will emerge most powerfully in actual, real-life practice settings. Active professional learning needs to be both facilitated and encouraged.

Ongoing support for professional development

Evidence from a range of sources suggests that professional members of joined-up teams experience shifts in professional identities and are constantly challenged in terms of the boundaries they work within and the changing practices they adopt. Professional skills and knowledge are exchanged and distributed among those working together. Chapter 6 described examples of professionals' informal learning at work. Informal learning happens spontaneously and can be as productive in promoting professional development as formal training, but managers need to find ways to support and enable these profound learning experiences, situated in the daily working lives of the team members.

Paying attention to 'specialist' skills retention

Workers in joined-up teams sometimes feel that their skills and expertise are undermined when there is an emphasis on team workers becoming generalists.

Some felt that their professional identity would be undermined and that promotion opportunities in mainstream work could be damaged. Farmakopoulou (2002: 1052) argues that the motivation to collaborate tends to be internal to each organization. The best inter-organizational relations exist when members perceive mutual benefits from interacting with and sharing skills and knowledge with other professionals.

Conclusion

In this chapter we have made some tentative suggestions arising from the implications of our work for decision-making and service delivery. In the final part of this book we explore a range of challenges facing multi-professional working with children and young people.

Think point

If you work in a multi-disciplinary setting, complete the checklist in the Appendix of this book. What have you learnt from completing the checklist? What can you apply to your practice and/or your learning?

Part 4

Contemporary challenges in multi-professional work with children and young people

In this part of the book we explore a range of contemporary challenges in multi-professional child welfare work: issues explored include leadership and assessment, information-sharing, children with Special Educational Needs, and challenging child sexual exploitation.

9

Safeguarding children: leadership and integrated assessment

Julie Jenkins and Melanie John-Ross

Introduction

The aim of this chapter is to set out the policy context for integrated children's services, the barriers and what contributes to the effective leadership of public services. Specifically we consider the challenge of leading integrated services and the roles of the director of children's services (DCS) and lead elected member for children in local authority areas. This discussion is then embedded in the learning from a case study of the development of integrated assessment services to protect children in a large metropolitan district.

Background

The drive to integrate children's services became a priority for the Labour government following the Lord Laming Inquiry (2003) into a child death. The inquiry reported what it saw as poor leadership, a lack of accountability and a chasm in senior officers' understanding of their responsibility to deliver joined-up, effective children's services. Partially in response to this the then New Labour government launched 'Every Child Matters' (DfES 2003), an ambitious change programme setting a national framework to improve outcomes for children. Statute followed with the Children Act 2004 requiring all councils to appoint a DCS. This post was unique as it combined for the first time leadership of all local authority children's services, including schools. The Act also required every top tier local authority to designate one of its members as the lead member for children's services.

The lead member is a local councillor with delegated responsibility from the council for children's services. As a member of the council executive they have political responsibility for the leadership, strategy and effectiveness of local authority children's services.

The DCS is a chief officer post with significant power and many responsibilities: these include being a system leader, change-maker and professional champion. DCSs orchestrate a wide range of activities, people and agencies, many of whom they do not manage. The DCS has a major leadership role for children's services, and is expected to drive cultural change and make sure that new partnerships improve service delivery. These are high expectations of one individual to overcome the challenge to work together, one of the eternal problems of both central and local government. This chapter will embed these wider developments by analysing the development of integrated assessment teams in children's social care: asking what the barriers are to integrated working and exploring to what extent they can be addressed; and exploring whether we set our leaders up to fail in expecting them to find solutions to complex, 'wicked' problems and ultimately holding them personally to account for system failure.

Context and policy background

Developments since 2003: policy and structural solutions

The leadership of integrated children's services has become a major political and policy priority following repeated high profile child protection failures. Following a child death, Lord Laming was asked by the government to carry out a review and make recommendations to improve the safeguarding of children in England. Laming (2003: 3–6) found that agencies cannot work effectively alone, services were often poorly led and the accountability for failure rested with managers and senior leaders. He argued that the most important change must be the drawing of a clear line of accountability, from top to bottom, and described effective leadership as requiring clear values, an ability to 'lead from the front' and a focus on outcomes, not bureaucratic activity. He did not recommend investment into services, but instead urged statutory agencies to become more outward-looking, flexible in the way they work and to utilize their resources more effectively (Laming 2003: 361).

The New Labour government at the time agreed that integrating children's services was a high priority and launched the Green Paper, *Every Child Matters* (DfES 2003). Local authorities were for the first time to bring together in one place, crucially under one person, services for children. The intention was to create the post of DCS, accountable for integrated local authority children's services and for improving the lives of children and young people. This was an ambitious 10-year change programme (Frost and Parton 2009). The White Paper, *Every Child Matters: Change for Children* (DfeS 2004) stressed the expectation that the DCS, with the lead member for children, would lead transformational change across local services.

The Children Act 2004 provided the legal basis, requiring all councils to appoint a DCS. The DCS is a chief officer post, responsible for the 'Children's Service Authority', combining the local authority's functions, including early years' services, education, social care and the youth service. The DCS is a powerful position, potentially controlling large percentages of council budgets and staff. The DCS and lead member are responsible for leading the statutory duty for partners to cooperate with each other, in order to develop effective integrated children's services. By bringing services under two leadership figures, the aim was to reduce the barriers to effective integrated, multi-professional delivery of services to children in need.

The role of the DCS

The statutory guidance (DfE 2013) on the roles and responsibilities of the DCS states they must work closely together with the lead elected member for children to provide the clear and unambiguous top line of accountability for children's well-being. The DCS leadership role requires holding partners to account for their duty to cooperate and integrate council services. This guidance has significantly watered down the New Labour 2009 guidance which called for the DCS, with the lead member, to champion the integration of services at the front line, in multi-agency teams and co-located services, and ensure that individual schools were engaged in the change process and improvement. The 2013 guidance takes into account the changing nature of relationships with 'free' schools and academies, which have degrees of independence from local authority control.

The 2013 guidance asks the DCS to target the 'hard to reach' and 'narrow the gap' for disadvantaged groups, with a strong emphasis on creating and sustaining effective local partnerships. A key leadership task is for the DCS to drive forward the cultural, workforce and other changes necessary to ensure services cohere around children's needs. This task requires putting children at the centre of service provision rather than building it around organizations and professional disciplines. Not only must the DCS provide strong leadership themselves but they must also ensure that there is clear leadership at all levels of children's services across the local authority, including in schools. This is challenging given the freedom and encouragement by the government for schools to be more independent and locally managed, and the relative power of headteachers. The total role amounts to high expectations of one individual leader to bring together a range of professionals to deliver integrated children's services.

Barriers to integration

The drive for the government to integrate services is well laid out in Perri 6 et al. (2002: 9). They assert that the joining up, coordination and integration of services is an 'eternal' if not *the* 'eternal' problem of local governance. The problems of fragmentation are set out by Perri 6 et al. (2002: 39–40): first, the dumping of problems and costs by one agency on another; focusing on one agency's priorities can leave the other picking up the pieces. For example, if schools exclude a young person for poor behaviour the young person is more likely to become involved in youth crime and even become 'looked after' by the local authority. Second, conflicting policy goals are still in place for many children's service agencies. Third, duplication can cause wasted resources and frustration to families who have to undergo repeated assessments and processes.

Differing agency responses to families' needs, inaccessibility and gaps in services are all problems associated with fragmentation and inherited, backward-looking sets of professional interventions. Perri 6 et al. (2005) describe and outline poor sequencing and a lack of appropriate interventions by professionals; this happens when there is a lack of communication and a failure to identify early need. Fragmentation can then lead to families accessing specialist services, with avoidable and poor outcomes, as evidenced by the disproportionate amount of children in care who end up in prison (DCSF 2007b).

The challenge for leaders to integrate services around the needs of children and families can be seen as a 'wicked issue', as described by Stewart (1997: 19). 'Wicked issues' are intractable problems which require tackling by holistic thinking, working outside organizational boundaries, involving the public in developing new service responses and a willingness to work in a completely new way.

The challenges to integrated children's services have been identified by Robinson et al. (2008: vii). These are grouped together under four main themes. Firstly, contextual barriers and political climate, when there are changes in political 'steer', reorganizations, financial uncertainty and local needs are at odds with national priorities. Secondly, organizational challenges such as different policies, procedures and obstacles to information-sharing. Thirdly, cultural and professional differences and negative professional stereotyping. The fourth theme identified by Robinson et al. is that real ownership is not embedded, and integrated working is vulnerable to changes in priorities and not seen as part of the core work.

Effective leadership of public services

Given these 'wicked issues' and the barriers to integrated services it can be argued that new models of leadership are required in order to break out of old behaviours and failed systems. Chesterman and Horne (2002) argue that leadership of public services is of the utmost importance with partnerships as places where the learning, thinking and development of creative solutions to intractable social problems are found. They agree that many of the social problems that affect families and communities have widespread roots, spreading across the domain of different agencies, professions and localities. They argue against focusing on the quality of individual leaders and instead prefer to concentrate on the relationships between service, professionals and communities. This is encouraged by suspending the specific interests of the respective institutions so that the possibility of organizing differently can be explored.

Chesterman and Horne argue that local authorities have a unique role in mediating between the state and communities: suspending the specific identity of individual services can increase social capital by building on the strengths of families and communities. Simply joining up the visible parts of a fragmented service is not enough – organizations need permeable boundaries and professions that value the knowledge of those they serve and work with. They see the main way to achieve these goals as being through the ancient and easy way to cultivate conditions for change: that is, by talking to people and engaging with them. This requires informal shared time between the DCS, service users, partners and staff at the front line.

Research for the Northern Leadership Academy by Maltby (2007) outlines two further styles to enhance our understanding of leadership in modern complex public sector organizations and systems:

- *Distributed leadership*: requires leadership as part of a wider leadership capability where the social capital of an organization is harnessed. The impact of a headteacher for example is mediated by staff, parents and the wider community. By working together they can have more impact on a student's performance.

- *System leadership*: this takes us out of the realms of organizational boundaries into leadership that takes place in multiple systems. Leaders connect the system through dialogue and feedback and sustain systems that make the most of capacity and the capacity to adapt. Leaders make decisions that are congruent with the purpose and articulated values of the whole system (Maltby 2007: 8–9).

The challenge of leading integrated children's services

Atkinson et al. (2007: 56) argue that leadership is a key factor in implementing effective integration. Leadership and drive at a strategic level, including vision and tenacity, enhance multi-agency working. Frost and Lloyd (2006: 13) agree and describe effective leadership as being challenging yet essential for developing effective integrated working, requiring individuals who can work in the new and ever-changing world of integration that involves intensive networking and boundary crossing. Frost and Lloyd argue that senior managers must be strongly personally committed to partnership work and that this is a major factor in achieving integration.

The National Evaluation of Children's Trusts Pathfinders (NECTP 2007: 3) identified that influence and negotiation are characteristics of effective leadership in networked organizations. Negotiation skills are highlighted as being essential in engaging stakeholders, but particularly challenging when working with headteachers and general practitioners who hold considerable power and autonomy in their own right. A drive at the strategic level is required, and vision and tenacity were instrumental in putting successful partnerships in place.

Lownsborough and O'Leary (2005) write that the DCS role is to be welcomed; it will have its part to play in reshaping integrated children's services. However, the creation of a new leadership position brings with it the risk of propping up an unsustainable model of leadership where leaders are repeatedly set up to fail. Integrated services require leaders who pursue solutions to often complex and deeply ingrained problems. Despite the repeated failure of a range of leaders, Lownsborough and O'Leary argue that we do not question our understanding of leadership, but tend to project our disappointment onto the individuals in charge. This is evidenced in the dismissal and resignation of several directors of children's services, Haringey and Rotherham being two high profile examples (*Guardian* 2009; BBC News 2014). They argue against structural and other solutions and believe the focus should be on bringing about cultural change. This process requires skills in aligning different sets of professional values, acknowledging that there will be different responses from professional groups and differences in the pace that change will be accepted. Lownsborough and O'Leary argue that successful change is managed through leaders being clear at the beginning and throughout the change process and also by managing and finding practical ways of addressing professionals' concerns and fears.

However, Lord et al. (2008) found in their research that 50 per cent of the DCSs interviewed indicated that there was no consensus on an integrated children's service definition in their authority. There was no shared understanding and a 'greyness about how people interpret integrated children's services' (2008: 7).

The implications of leading an integrated children's workforce are explored by Frost (2009) who says there are many challenges involved in the role. Most leaders will have had until recently a specific professional identity, perhaps as an educationalist or a social worker, and will have led organizations dominated by a single profession. The world of integrated services brings professions together under the Children's Trust arrangements. This creates a leadership challenge of generating a shared professional identity and agreed goals. Professions have to adopt an increasingly integrated and holistic view of childhood and leaders must have credibility to speak across and beyond traditional organizational boundaries. Frost states that in facing these challenges it is crucial that children's service leaders are flexible, responsive and inventive: he argues that an effective DCS needs to build a team of leaders. Frost (2009) concludes that even the most talented leaders require the input and leadership of others, constructively solicited, and creatively applied.

Strong leadership and management are vital to success according to Robinson et al. (2008: 78). Leaders need to be aware of the emotional processes around change and this in turn places emotional demands on them. They argue that emotional intelligence is important in new leadership roles and the development of partnerships. However, where integrated children's services are reliant on the drive and motivation of one key individual, the DCS, this raises questions about sustainability.

In 2014, Solace (which represents local authority chief executives) produced an influential report about the future of children's services and the DCS role. In the report, *Reclaiming Children's Services*, it is argued that local authority child protection services do not operate in a vacuum as schools, GP surgeries, communities and voluntary providers all have a crucial part to play in keeping children safe. Serious case reviews and inquiries have highlighted the need for collaborative working and good communication. In response, many local authorities have brought councils, police and others together in specialist integrated settings dealing with referral, assessment and triage.

Solace (2014: 12–13) also highlights the national concerns arising from the high turnover of DCS positions. The turnover rate during 2012–13 totalled almost a third. Solace argues that this instability arises fundamentally from a 'blame culture' where accountability is seen as the responsibility of a single individual. Solace believes that the chief executive of local authorities along with the leader, political leaders and the corporate team have crucial roles to play in children's services.

So to summarize the literature on leadership of integrated children's services: a leader best placed to overcome barriers to integrated services will use a collection of styles with a focus on transformational approaches to change. They will harness the capacity of the system and the distributed power of the senior team and partnership. Boundary-spanning techniques should be used to tackle a range of 'wicked issues'. A DCS needs to be emotionally intelligent, using conversations, networking and the quality of relationships to effect change, rather than structures, meetings and formalized processes.

The development of a multi-agency assessment team – integrated working in child protection

So in the application of transformative models of integrated working to safeguard children, can integrated services in child protection work break down professional barriers, improve outcomes and assure the single lines of accountability (DCS and lead member) that children are safe? In this section we report a case study that was undertaken to understand the experience, impact and learning from the implementation of a multi-disciplinary children's assessment team in a large English metropolitan district with high levels of deprivation. The Children's Trust in this area had identified integrated services as a high priority. This goal was set out in a Children and Young People's Plan and had the 'buy in' and ownership of the DCS and lead member, in addition to the senior leaders across the council, NHS, third sector and the police.

As part of this process, a multi-disciplinary integrated assessment team was developed against a background of growing public and professional awareness of the learning from public inquiries into child deaths. This had led to increased referrals to this council's children's social care services. Munro (2011c) confirms that this was a national problem with high referral rates to such services. The first problem is that on close examination many families do not necessarily need a service from children's social care, despite having been referred and put through potentially unnecessary assessments and intrusive enquiries into their parenting. The second challenge is that assessing referrals is resource intensive and such resources would be far more effective if responding to more appropriate referrals for children and young people who are at risk of harm. Munro concludes with the view, as pioneered under the Every Child Matters programme (DfES 2003), that prevention and early help by universal services is key to meeting children's unmet needs, preventing need from escalating into risk of harm and the social care remit.

As a means of addressing this issue, the local authority that was the subject of the research introduced a multi-disciplinary assessment team to support professionals in facilitating alternative interventions for those children who were not judged to be at risk of harm. The aim of the new integrated assessment team was to improve information-sharing and communication across agencies and deliver integrated responses to referrals to children's social care. The team sought to promote early help interventions and services where these were more appropriate, by providing advice and consultation to professional referrers working in universal services. This was in order to support them in working with vulnerable children and managing lower levels of risk.

The police, health and education services each seconded practitioners into the team, which was managed and hosted by the local authority. The seconded professionals remained employed by their employing agency and were located with social workers to form the integrated assessment team. The team worked under the agreed local Safeguarding Children Board safeguarding procedures.

The experience of these multi-professional practitioners working in the integrated assessment team was evaluated using a case study approach: the data collection method was to conduct semi-structured individual interviews with members of the team. The findings were evaluated against the findings from a literature review of the context of child protection and multi-agency team models.

Key findings: pressures, challenges and positive experiences in the integrated assessment team

The case study identified the benefits, pressures and challenges experienced by the group and gave an insight into their own understanding of the integrated assessment team. The co-location of the integrated assessment team involved all practitioners having access to their own organization's electronic recording systems and the sharing of information was positive and not reported to be an issue or barrier by any member of the group (see Chapter 11 of this book). This is in contrast to the findings in repeated serious case reviews (Brandon et al. 2008).

The timely ease of sharing information across the agencies represented in the team was reported as a real benefit by the entire interview sample. This is extremely important within child protection, given that poor inter-agency communication is cited as a reoccurring theme within serious case reviews into child deaths, where abuse or neglect is suspected (see Rose and Barnes 2008; see also Brandon et al. 2008).

A challenge experienced by the team was professionals being clear about their agency role and responsibilities, with sufficient seniority to facilitate conversations with referrers. The health professionals had a high level of training and child protection expertise and could advise colleagues on how to manage levels of risk in the community with their support. Health is a large organization and there will be power dynamics between the different professionals who hold varying status. However, with sufficient child protection training health visitors can be confident in challenging doctors and paediatricians, breaking down leadership barriers.

In contrast, the education social work service staff, who were qualified professional social workers, felt inhibited by the informal rules within their profession and the perceived power imbalance between the social work education service and qualified teachers and the headteachers. This may reflect the fact that education services are delivered across many different settings and that headteachers are largely autonomous and in control of their school and its ethos. While schools are clearly subject to regulated inspection by Ofsted, they are not directly managed by the local authority. For the education welfare staff, the status and role of headteachers and teachers acted as a barrier to them fulfilling their role to help schools to consider alternative interventions for families, where there were no child protection concerns.

The police have an invaluable role fulfilling the task of sharing information from their intelligence systems and screening police domestic violence notifications to the team. Their primary responsibility, together with children's social care, is conducting joint child protection assessments. Arrangements for assessing and investigating child protection concerns are set out under the statutory guidance, *Working Together to Safeguard Children* (DfE 2013), which makes clear the requirement for strategy discussions between children's social care and the police immediately upon child protection referrals being received. Integrated assessment teams require a police officer from a child protection background who can fulfil this role and provide a co-located joint approach to investigation. This research identified that the most effective use of police capacity is to have the right level of experience and rank of officer to undertake both these tasks and roles.

The social workers identified high referrals to children's social care as problematic and they agreed with Munro's (2011c) analysis that many of these were inappropriate and not child protection. Their reasons were twofold. The first was that high referrals equated to high workloads for them. However, the main reason they saw this as an issue was that children were being inappropriately referred and families experienced unnecessary and intrusive assessments by children's social care. This can be stigmatizing and stressful for families. Where the assessments concluded that the child was not at risk of significant harm but could benefit from universal preventative services, this raised the issue of why this could not have been identified and responded to beforehand, by early help services.

Social workers also identified as a pressure having to log everything and every call from any referrer, even when both they and the referrer recognized that it was actually not a valid referral. They reported that this was time intensive and that consequently more time was spent recording and inputting this data than in any direct contact with a referrer or family. This risk averse and 'back covering' behaviour takes valuable time away from actually protecting the children that need it.

Local authority children's social care services are the lead statutory agency for assessing risk to children, as set out under the Children Act 1989 and the statutory guidance *Working Together to Safeguard Children* (DfE 2013). This statutory guidance, as well as the Children Act 2004 also makes clear the safeguarding responsibilities of all agencies who provide services to children, which includes referring them to children's social care services where they suspect a child is being neglected or harmed.

Therefore, there is a clear responsibility for professionals working with children to report their concerns to children's social care, but high profile child deaths have promoted an anxiety among professionals, leading to referrals that do not progress into direct services. Children's social care record all information that is reported to them, as the social workers in the group commented upon. This is because a single piece of information may be relevant when analysed against previous or future information that is recorded, building up a picture of the care of a child. Both practices, the reporting of all information and the recording of it, could be argued to be defensive practice and practice that has been developed in response to reported serious cases. Ultimately this is very safe practice, but there is a danger of the most risky cases getting 'lost' in the large number of inappropriate contacts. As Munro states: 'The understandable public distress when a child dies, leading to the castigation of the workers involved, is a continuing driver of defensive practice that fails to prioritise the child's best interests' (2011c: 94).

An understanding of what works

The study did provide an understanding of what works in front-line integrated practice. The issue of high referrals to children's social care services and the importance of prevention and early help for children is well set out by Munro in her review of child protection (2011c). An overall aim of the integrated team is to support as much appropriate help at an early stage for families before the need for specialist intervention.

In this study there was successful collaboration between social work, health staff and the police. Social workers referred in their interviews to working 'in partnership' and 'speaking a common language', which they clarified as being child protection language. Staff from different agencies described working as equals and felt that the other agencies had something to offer to an understanding of the family situation and functioning. When it works well the practitioners have a shared understanding of reducing inappropriate referrals to the team and supporting agencies in finding alternative family interventions. Respect for each other had been won by undertaking joint visits and assessments and supporting each other with difficult circumstances such as the removal of children from their family.

One of the social workers spoke about the 'right person for the job', suggesting that behaviour, and communication and relationships skills, influenced the effectiveness of practitioners in an integrated team. These 'tacit' skills supplemented the more 'explicit' skills relating to their formal professional role and expertise. Understanding informal roles is as important as defining the formal professional roles within an integrated team, as perceptions and beliefs in respect of status and power will affect how effective practitioners are in their roles and in their interactions with both internal and external colleagues.

Practitioners who are working across organizations and across professional roles also need clear support in respect of leadership and management, given the tensions that exist between agencies and different priorities. In this case, agencies were wanting to pass their concerns for children on to children's social care, who were in turn wanting to pass them back where there was no evidence of child protection issues.

Conclusion

Forming a multi-disciplinary and integrated assessment team is clearly not just about seconding professionals from one agency into another. It requires consideration of the professional background, experience and skills of the practitioners, and the role and duties they will perform, matched against the purpose and function of the team that is to become integrated. However, as Dan Parton concluded, 'it takes time to build an integrated team – you can't just assume that by putting people together it will automatically work' (Parton 2008: 9).

Organizational restraints, in respect of limited resources, procedures and rules need to be explored to understand how they influence the role, function and effectiveness of an integrated team if barriers are to be addressed and resolved. The challenge that education welfare staff experienced in how they related to education colleagues in schools was actually the same as the social workers, who reported high referral rates due to 'different agency agendas, procedures and clashing priorities' (Frost et al. 2005: 193). Therefore, understanding agencies' different and conflicting agendas and priorities is important for integrated teams.

Leadership is vital to establish the team and overcome resource restraints. Sharing information, real-time communication and joint approaches help to protect children. This can be seen in the evident learning from serious case reviews. Communicating clear expectations of the team, its aims and objectives, assists in clarifying the different roles within it and their relationship with these objectives, as well as with one another.

All the involved practitioners need the continued support of their strategic leaders, as shifts towards integration and co-location can be challenged in times of austerity. The commitment and leadership from the DCS and lead member sets the vision and priority for inter-agency strategic partnerships, such as the local Safeguarding Children Board and the local Children's Trust. They have a key role in creating ownership of the promotion of early help and intervention by children's universal services, which is necessary to reduce unnecessary referrals to children's social care and keep children safe with their families in their community.

Think points

- How is leadership of multi-professional organizations different from leading single professional organizations?
- What are the advantages and disadvantages of integrated assessment teams?

10

Joining it up: multi-professional information-sharing

Sue Richardson

Introduction

This chapter introduces four theoretical approaches to the challenge of multi-professional information-sharing in public service delivery. Two of the four approaches are then described in more detail as lenses through which to explore what happens in the practice of integrated children's services. The two approaches explored in detail are the systems approach and the approach that underpins much of this book: Etienne Wenger's 'communities of practice'.

The focus of the chapter is on the professionals delivering the services and not primarily on the children, young people or their families who are in receipt of these services. This approach however is in no way antagonistic to the idea that it is the interests of the children and young people that must always come first when redesigning organizations, policies, procedures and guidance for practice in children's services.

Before moving on to the substance of the chapter, the following points establish the scope and structure of the argument:

- 'Integrated' in this chapter is construed broadly, to include all situations where more than one profession, service or organization works together in delivering a service in such a way as the users of the service see it as just that – a service – and not a number of separate services. It is not restricted to situations where the services have been formally integrated to the extent of becoming a single legal entity.

- Although the context for the chapter is integrated children's services, much of what is presented is generally applicable to the sharing of personal, sensitive information in the delivery of any public service.

- There are many forms of information-sharing and only one is considered here – that is the sharing of personal, and often sensitive, information between those working in multi-professional teams in integrated children's services. This might be sharing within the team or with other practitioners or officers in other services, across professional, organizational, sectoral, service or agency boundaries. Other forms, for example sharing of large data-sets, sharing of information for research purposes and sharing between practitioner and service user, do not come within the remit of this chapter.

- There are important distinctions to be made between 'data', 'information' and 'knowledge'. The contexts relevant to the chapter are mostly concerned with data and information and for the current purpose no significant distinction is made between these. The term most commonly used will be 'information-sharing' but on occasions there will also be reference to data-sharing, particularly in relation to the work of other authors who have utilized this term.

- Regarding the legal and policy aspects of information-sharing in children's services, it is the English legal system and policy context that is considered here.

The challenge of information-sharing

The challenge of information-sharing lies in the requirement of practitioners to simultaneously achieve two goals that can be seen as conflicting: to share personal information across professional, organizational, sectoral, service or agency boundaries while at the same time protecting it so that confidentiality is not breached. This conflict has been heightened in recent years with encouragement being given, through varieties of 'public service transformation', for a greater level of integration across services.

As practitioners are aware, there are two compelling reasons for ensuring that information is protected by public service agencies. One is that breaking confidence unnecessarily can have devastating consequences for the individuals whose personal information has been shared (as well as for those close to them). The second is that unless people trust that information they tell public service professionals is held in confidence, they will be less likely to seek help (including treatment) or to give full information. This has implications for the well-being of individuals and it can also be important for the general population. For example, when someone begins to hear voices, if they are reluctant to go to their general practitioner because they fear that information about their mental health will not be kept confidential, their condition could get worse without treatment, and could conceivably result in them harming themselves or someone else.

Equally, there are important reasons to share information. Not sharing can put the care of an individual service user at risk, for instance because a practitioner with caring responsibilities does not have a complete picture of their situation. It can also pose risks beyond the individual – for example, failing to share a service user's information across organizational boundaries could result in harm to others. Thus there is a tension between sharing and protecting information. Entangled with this first tension is another: that between risks to the individual and risks to the wider community. As will be shown later, this can become important for understanding some of the problems that arise in information-sharing.

This challenge of sharing personal service user information is faced by public service professionals, whether they work in health, social services, education, criminal justice, housing, employment services, or others, and whether they work in the statutory, voluntary or private sector. Practitioners frequently describe meeting this challenge as 'walking a tightrope'. Public services need to ensure that information vital to the well-being of an individual, a family or a community is passed on to all professionals who need to be informed, while at the same time taking care that information held about a service user is not shared inappropriately or without good cause, thus maintaining data privacy and confidentiality. The stakes are high: falling off the tightrope on either side can result in tragedy.

Theoretical approaches to the challenge

So, what theoretical approaches have been employed in attempts to understand information-sharing in practice? This section provides a brief overview of these theories.

A neo-Durkheimian institutional approach has been proposed (Perri 6 et al. 2005). In this approach a range of social theories are utilized to explain or predict which of four 'types' or 'zones' of institution, dependent on levels of social integration and of social regulation, will have a greater or lesser 'willingness' (or 'capacity') to share data or a higher or lower disposition towards the 'rejection' of data-sharing.

One of the main difficulties for application to practice of such an approach is that there is an inherent assumption that the goal should be information-sharing. The theory was devised to account for the observation that despite policy encouragement to do so, some agencies still seemed reluctant to embrace information-sharing, and so the focus on the degree of sharing is perhaps not surprising. Arguably, however, much more important than asking about the level of information-sharing is querying how appropriate the sharing practice is and how appropriate the rejection of information-sharing is, at the level of each potential information-sharing interaction.

Later, this same team of researchers employed a risk management approach to study, that they call 'information sharing dilemmas' (Perri 6 et al. 2010). They identified four configurations of information-sharing contexts dependent on (a) whether the services involved are universal or targeted and (b) whether they primarily benefit individuals or third parties/wider society. The four configurations are as follows: universal for the benefit of individuals; universal for the benefit of third parties or the general public; selective for the benefit of individuals; and selective for the benefit of third parties or the general public. Each of the four tends to handle different kinds of information and in different ways. The model highlights the complexities that need to be considered and the dangers of relying on simplistic algorithms for information-sharing decision-taking in order to 'balance' the risks of sharing (disclosing) with those of withholding (protecting) information.

The idea is that risk in information-sharing can never be completely eliminated although some risk-based heuristics could be helpful in developing policy. The point is also made that government policy is more tolerant of false positive errors (too much information-sharing) at some times and more tolerant of false negative errors (too little information-sharing) at others, and that this needs to be openly acknowledged so that practitioners can be supported when errors occur (Perri 6 et al. 2010: 479). A risk management approach to sharing information, incorporating the idea of a tension between the interests of individuals and groups, has also been employed by Barton and Quinn (2002) in the domain of drug treatment and criminal justice.

Several authors have engaged with information-sharing through a systems approach (see for example Richardson and Asthana 2005, 2006: Dawes et al. 2009; Baines, et al. 2010; Yang and Maxwell 2011; Eason and Waterson 2013; Dent and Tutt 2014; Wastell and White 2014). Those who have chosen to use a systems approach frequently do so because they want their readers to remember that all the interacting elements affecting the subject of study are dependent on each other: change one and almost certainly there will be consequences in unexpected places.

The final approach considered here actually draws heavily on systems theory, and in the study of information-sharing it can in some ways be thought of as a specific form of the systems approach. This is the communities of practice approach which we first introduced in Chapter 1. Lave and Wenger (1991) first proposed 'communities of practice' as a way of understanding how apprentices learned their trade. The ideas were further elaborated in Etienne Wenger's book *Communities of Practice: Learning, Meaning and Identity* (1998). Wenger's notion of communities of practice provides an excellent set of frameworks, as well as a language, for tackling the complexities of information-sharing. It assumes that we do not have to be constrained or restricted by the conventional boundaries of profession, organization, service and agency. What can be more productive is to think of the different communities of practice at work and to ask questions of these communities. What is important to people working in them? How are they similar and different? What clusters or 'constellations' of communities of practice are there and what are the implications of these?

What makes a community of practice different from other communities is that, in a community of practice, practice is the source of coherence of the community (Wenger 1998: 72). To recap from Chapter 1, there are three dimensions of practice that, as the property of a community, provide this coherence:

- mutual engagement;
- a joint enterprise;
- a shared repertoire.

After giving some examples of using a systems approach to investigate information-sharing, it is the communities of practice approach that will then infuse the remainder of this chapter.

Using a systems approach to explore information-sharing

This section draws on research undertaken in two Sure Start Children's Centres. One of the aims of the research project was to identify the factors influencing how practitioners share service user information across organizational boundaries (Richardson 2007).

The research took the level of 'the system' to be that of the organization, agency or the service that the practitioner was working in (some services being delivered across a number of organizations). This might be within the public, private or voluntary and community sectors. The 'supra-system' level of the wider environment and the 'sub-system' level of the individual practitioner were also explored. One representation of influencing factors that were found is shown in Figure 10.1. It can be seen from Figure 10.1 that there are multiple interdependent influences operating at different levels that affect whether, in a specific context, a practitioner shares (discloses) or withholds (protects) a service user's information. None of these factors can be considered in isolation.

This approach works by focusing on the individual potential information-sharing interaction between practitioners (the circle at the centre of Figure 10.1).

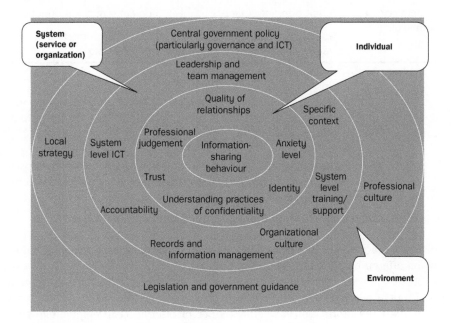

Figure 10.1 Information-sharing in context

Within an integrated children's service context, this might be, for example, an information-sharing interaction between a social worker and a health visitor within the service, or it might be between a social worker within the service and a health visitor outside, or between a social worker within the service and a social worker outside, and so on. Of course, many different services and professions might be involved, including those in children's and adult services, involving a variety of health services and professions, and those working in education, criminal justice, employment, housing and many more.

Although practitioners are making choices about sharing information all the time, they often do not consider in a systematic way the choices that are available to them and what might be influencing their decision-making. Table 10.1 shows the eight possibilities that are available in any potential information-sharing interaction.

Table 10.1 Information-sharing interactions

Type of Interaction	I hold service user Information	Another agency/service/ organization holds service user information
Sharing/ disclosing	I offer information	I request information
	I share/disclose if information is requested from me	I accept if information is offered to me
Protecting/ withholding	I do not offer information	I do not request information
	I protect/withhold if information is requested from me	I refuse if information is offered to me

When practitioners see this list, they frequently express surprise because some of the options available to them are rarely considered. The most 'forgotten' of the possible interactions are:

- offering service user information to a practitioner working outside their own organization, service or agency (although this is now becoming more common, even when safeguarding is not an issue);
- refusing service user information offered by another practitioner.

For many practitioners, the potentially negative consequences of accepting information offered by another agency has not been a prime consideration. However, of course, when seen with the other possibilities, it becomes clear that information should not be accepted without clarifying various issues. These might include: what the source of the information is; whether the person offering it can legitimately share it; the accuracy of the information; whether only the information that is needed for the particular purpose in question is being offered (rather than, for instance, the rest of the spreadsheet or case record that it is taken from); and so on.

Table 10.1 shows that half of the possible interactions are sharing (or disclosing) interactions and half of them are protecting (or withholding) interactions. The research proposed that, theoretically, any of the interactions made by an individual practitioner, whether sharing or protecting, could be either appropriate (with good cause) or inappropriate.

What is classified as 'good cause' is relatively clear in a potential safeguarding situation, but can be harder to assess in other contexts. It is usually impossible to know in practice if the decisions are appropriate or not, unless there is a problem in the future as a consequence of the decision. Lack of such feedback could be one reason why developing this kind of professional judgement can be very difficult.

Assuming that a practitioner will sometimes share and sometimes withhold information, the research proposed a 'model of appropriate information sharing interactions' based on the logical possibilities (Richardson and Asthana 2005). A two by two matrix with an 'appropriate/inappropriate' dimension and a 'sharing/protecting interactions' dimension gives four quadrants:

- The 'ideal': information is shared appropriately but is equally withheld when there is good cause to do so. Low risk of breaching confidentiality and low risk of neglecting to pass on important information.

- The 'over-open': information is withheld appropriately but information is shared without good cause. High risk of breaching confidentiality and low risk of neglecting to pass on important information.

- The 'over-cautious': information is shared appropriately but information is withheld without good cause. Low risk of breaching confidentiality but high risk of neglecting to pass on important information.

- The 'chaotic': information is shared inappropriately and is also withheld without good cause. High risk both of breaching confidentiality and of neglecting to pass on important information.

The research aimed to identify what might facilitate an individual practitioner (or indeed an organization, service or agency), moving towards the 'ideal' situation where all information-sharing interactions, whether they result in exchange of information or not, are appropriate. It used a series of interviews with practitioners to explore the influences in Figure 10.1 and their relation to the 'ideal' and the other three categories of information-sharing interaction.

The findings suggested that there was one factor capable of moderating both a tendency of practitioners to be 'over-cautious' in their information-sharing interactions and their tendency to be 'over-open', so facilitating a move towards the 'ideal' (Richardson 2007). Other potential influencing factors investigated were found to be capable of moderating in one direction or the other but either of these holds inherent risks. Increasing personal trust between practitioners for example can moderate over-cautiousness but it can then lead to information being shared when it should not be, in other words becoming 'over-open'.

The one thing that seemed to help prevent both over-cautiousness and over-openness was an understanding of how practitioners in other professions or services work with confidentiality of service user information. This is what can be seen as others' 'practices of confidentiality' and the idea will be returned to in the discussion of communities of practice.

The communities of practice approach and information-sharing

As previously stated, the trio of dimensions of practice that enable the coherence required for a community to be thought of as a community of practice comprise: mutual engagement, a joint enterprise and a shared repertoire. Anyone working in an integrated children's service will no doubt see some familiarity here. Even though the service might comprise people from different professions, and with different employers, sometimes from different sectors, there will be some mutual engagement; there will be shared practices through working together. There will also be joint enterprise and a shared repertoire; for example, there will be mutual accountability and a shared history with common jargon and so on.

We each are members of many communities of practice though, and this complicates the picture, while also shedding some light on the problems of information-sharing. To make sense of this, some other concepts fundamental to Wenger's vision of a community of practice need to be considered.

Participation and reification

For Wenger, meanings are arrived at through the continual flow and ebb of our social relations, of our living in the world. According to Wenger, fundamental to this 'negotiation of meaning' is the duality of 'participation' and 'reification' (1998: 55). Participation, in this technical sense, is probably easier to grasp than reification.

Participation is more than merely current physical engagement in a community of practice. Participation in the community stays with an individual, even when the individual is not physically engaging in the practice of the community. For example, when Jenny, a speech and language therapist, goes to the theatre with her partner in the evening, she remains a participant in several communities of practice: the smallish multi-professional team that comprises the integrated children's service she works in and the larger community of speech and language therapists that she feels part of through her professional networks and the local charity that employs her, from which she is seconded. The meaningfulness of this play that Jenny is watching, about the role of the state in terrorist activity, as well as the significance of the evening for her and her partner, will be coloured by her participation in these (and other) communities of practice.

According to Wenger, reification is 'the process of giving form to our experience by producing objects that congeal this experience into "thingness"' (1998: 58). Whenever a tool is produced, a form devised, a new term coined, then reification is happening. The products of reification can then become the focus for the negotiation of meaning. For those familiar with socio-technical systems theory, it is too easy to assume connections here. There are similarities, in that participation can be seen as related to the social system and reification can be seen as related to the technical system, but they are not equivalent. The pairing of participation and reification used in the communities of practice approach is located at both the level of community of practice and at the level of the individual in that the negotiation of meaning is constantly moving between the two.

It is impossible to separate participation and reification in Wenger's conception. However, it is often easy to simply accept that meanings are 'in' our behaviours or are 'in' things themselves. This can be dangerous as participation and reification can make up for the shortcomings in the other. An example is an information-sharing agreement, which, if well-constructed, can overcome some of the problems of poor communication between different agencies. On the other hand, if two practitioners from different agencies are required to make use of a poorly designed information-sharing agreement, they can overcome some of the resultant problems by developing a good working relationship and getting to know each other's processes and policies. This can illuminate some of the misunderstandings that might have surrounded the agreement.

Seen through the lens of communities of practice, the frustrations of practitioners around sharing information have changed over time. A market (or part market) economy was introduced into the delivery of public services in Margaret Thatcher's first period of government. Along with this came the 'new public management' needed to control and regulate it, and the inevitable partnership working needed to 'mend' the subsequent fracturing of services. These changes to service delivery led to a growing need to share information across boundaries. At this stage, there were complaints from practitioners that there was not enough guidance on information-sharing; there was insufficient reification. This was quickly followed not only by guidance from the Department for Constitutional Affairs (DCA 2003), which was intended to be the cross-government voice, but also from individual government departments, because they were involved with different communities of practice with both national and local boundaries. This resulted in too much contradictory guidance and much confusion and uncertainty for practitioners.

Multi-membership of communities of practice and constellations of practices

What is fascinating about most situations of information-sharing today is that they exist within a largely unrecognized multiplicity of different communities of practice. Wenger introduces two ways of thinking about such complexity. One is the 'multi-membership' of communities of practice (1998: 105) and the other is the idea of 'constellations' of practices (1998: 126).

Multi-membership uses the idea that people can participate in more than one community of practice and that reifications can be used by more than one community of practice. We have already met multi-membership when thinking about Jenny, the speech and language therapist. This clearly has implications for ideas of identity, which in turn can be important for information-sharing. Whether a practitioner relates more closely with the values of their profession, or the service they work in, or their employer organization, for example, might affect their practice of confidentiality, and also their understanding of others' practices of confidentiality.

 Multi-membership raises two relevant ideas borrowed from other authors. One is the concept of 'boundary brokers' (Burt 1992) to refer to specific roles that deliberately work across boundaries. A related term, 'boundary spanner', was introduced by Tushman (1977) and has been take up widely, but Wenger prefers 'broker'. Similarly, a 'boundary object' has been a useful notion, first proposed by Star and Griesemer (1989). A boundary object is a reification that might be used by a number of different communities of practice together in an agreed way but which is also used within each individual community of practice in its own localized manner.

A good example might be the English tool known as the Common Assessment Framework or CAF. There is a sense in which the CAF is used in an agreed ('central') way by multiple agencies within a locality. It is also true though, that when it is used by each of these agencies for its own purposes, there will be individual idiosyncrasies that are necessitated because of the different practices that are needed by each community of practice. The very word 'assessment' can even mean different things in different communities of practice. Understanding that boundary objects can have different meanings and be used in different ways in different communities of practice can help people to understand others' practices of confidentiality.

Constellations of practices work in a slightly different way from multi-membership of communities of practice. There could be constellations of practice within a single organization (often organizations include quite distinct communities of practice distinguished along professional or functional lines but which still act together as some form of unity) but, equally, we could look at an integrated service as either a community of practice in itself or as a constellation of interconnected practices, whether these relate to a set of organizational, professional, sectoral or service-related practices.

There is no hard 'fact of the matter' about the 'real' boundaries of these constellations. It is a question of whether people see the service as a community of practice, a constellation of practices or as a community of practice that is part of a larger constellation. What determines whether the integrated service is a community of practice or a constellation of practices is, in a sense, how integrated the service feels to those within it. Is there really mutual engagement? Does it feel as though boundaries are constantly being crossed within the service? Is there one shared repertoire, a common discourse in the service, or is communication via a generally agreeable set of distinct discourses? Are there individuals who are needed to work across boundaries and to engage in 'boundary practices'? The more it feels as though there are many boundaries inside, the more likely it is that there is a constellation of practices at work, rather than a community of practice.

As an example, there might be different kinds of communities of practice around 'Troubled Families' programmes (DCLG 2012), depending on how the programme is configured in different localities. In some places, this will work as an integrated service, focusing very much on the children in the family as long as the family meets the criteria for being part of the 'Troubled Families' programme. For other places, there might be a loose 'alliance' of services that have agreed to work together to deliver the programme. Where there is a more integrated service, it will work as a unit but it will be multi-professional and will still include close links with schools and other education services, job centres and other employment services, police and other criminal justice teams, as well as mainstream adults and children's services and health services. The kinds of question that need to be answered to determine whether this is a single community of practice or a constellation of practices are the following. Where do people within the service see their boundaries and how do people 'outside' the service see them? How strong, for example, is the identification of the front-line staff with the service compared with their identification with their profession or with the organizations they may have been seconded from?

Linking practices of confidentiality with communities of practice

As noted already, critical for the improvement of information-sharing can be the question of individuals' practice of confidentiality and this will depend to a large degree on the answers to the questions above. A front-line worker's practice of confidentiality seems to relate very much to the 'primary focus' of the practitioner. The practitioner might see their main allegiance as being to an individual service user. Alternatively, they may perceive their primary duty as being to the well-being of the family they are working with (in which case the needs of any one of the individuals in the family might have to take second place to the needs of the family as a whole). Similarly, their primary focus could be on the wider community, for example on public safety. In this case, the rights of an individual patient might need to be demoted in order to contain an epidemic of a contagious disease, or the rights of individuals might need to be temporarily curtailed to manage a potential terrorist threat.

A practitioner's community of practice, then, is a major 'shaper' of the practitioner's 'primary focus', and their 'primary focus' will largely determine their practices of confidentiality. When this is recognized, it can account for some of the antagonisms and misunderstandings that can sometimes emerge in information-sharing, where one professional judges another as acting wrongly because they do not share the same practice of confidentiality (Richardson and Asthana, 2006). Once it is understood that these differences can arise perfectly legitimately, and that they are in some ways inevitable because different professions and services are required to do different things in different ways, constructive communication between practitioners can be enabled in relation to the sharing of information. To summarize, understanding the reasons for variations in practices of confidentiality can be a key to better information-sharing and the communities of practice approach can be helpful for developing this understanding.

Improving information-sharing

Much of the chapter thus far has drawn attention to problems with information-sharing or with gaining a deeper understanding of the contexts of information-sharing, but with the implicit purpose of learning how to improve information-sharing. As has already been seen, *improving* information-sharing does not equate with *increasing* information-sharing, although, in some situations, improving information-sharing will coincide with increased information-sharing. It is the *quality* of information-sharing, however, that will be essential for improving service delivery.

There are emerging a number of exciting developments that could make a real difference to improving information-sharing. Unusually, compared with initiatives in the past, they are not driven by technological solutions but are rather being led more by ideas, such as those found in this chapter, around the importance of the ways in which people work together in different contexts.

Probably the most significant of these innovations is a government funded Centre of Excellence for Information Sharing (CEIS 2014). This is likely to become a key resource for all front-line practitioners as well as those working in information governance. The Centre, although funded from across government departments, is independent from government. It is likely to succeed where other initiatives to improve information-sharing have failed because it has thought carefully about how it should work and what its focus should be.

It is a virtual centre, with a small core staff, other centre members working in different localities across the country. Good practice of information-sharing on the ground will be gathered and shared across localities and will be recorded in the Centre. Good links are being nurtured with both local and central government so where there are barriers to good practice that originate at central government level, or which can only be removed by central government, there are links from the Centre into central government, providing an opportunity for blockages to be cleared.

Initiatives related to the Centre of Excellence are an Economic and Social Research Centre (ESRC) seminar series on information-sharing (to take place over three years to 2017) and an ESRC knowledge exchange project, 'Effective and Appropriate Sharing of Information' (EASI).

The EASI project had partners from the University of Bradford, Leeds Beckett University, the City of Bradford Metropolitan District Council and the government funded Improving Information Sharing and Management Project, the precursor to the CEIS. This project developed and piloted a multi-professional practitioner development programme called 'Valuing our Differences' made up of two one-day workshops, held a few weeks apart. It was designed to allow practitioners to gain a greater appreciation, within a locality, of the way in which different communities of practice, all involved in delivering public services, necessarily need to work differently from each other, and particularly to understand different practices of confidentiality.

Through the period of piloting the workshops (in Bradford District, Greater Manchester and in Leicestershire), a list of 'top tips' on information-sharing was slowly refined by the project leaders, with input from the workshop participants. The latest version is reproduced below in Box 10.1.

Box 10.1 Top tips

- Base your policy and practice within the legal requirements for information-sharing in general and your practice area specifically (1, 4)
- If you are starting a new project, programme or service, see if conducting a privacy impact assessment could help you to get things right from the start with respect to information-sharing (6)
- If a protocol and specific agreement under it does not already exist for the information-sharing you need to do, consider developing a protocol and agreement(s) for information-sharing for your organization if this will help reassure partners and/or your own information governance team, drawing on a clear vision of what is to be achieved (3)
- Ensure all staff members are fully aware of your protocols/agreements if you have them and provide training and human support in implementing and reviewing them (3, 5)
- Ensure your information and communications technology (ICT) system is secure and efficient in terms of information-sharing (1)
- Ensure all service user consent that is sought is fully recorded along with information-sharing decisions and their justification (1)
- In keeping with advice from the Information Commissioner's Office, if a legal gateway is available to you, consider this option before consent to share is sought (if consent is refused you may then find it hard to use the legal gateway) (2, 6)
- Ensure that information-sharing takes place only among those with a legitimate relationship (or potential legitimate relationship) with any concerned individual (1)

- Clearly explain to service users how information will be shared and with whom and under what circumstances it might be shared without consent (1)
- Clearly explain to service users how aggregate information might be used to inform research and policy development where relevant (1)
- Find out about other relevant agencies' protocols and thresholds and approaches to confidentiality; understand why they might be different from yours (4)
- Challenge when refusal to share information is inappropriate (4)
- Refuse information offered to you when sharing is inappropriate (4)
- Utilize the CEIS website and the Office of the Information Commissioner website to inform your information-sharing (see 2 and 6)
- Evaluate and gather evidence to achieve a clear feedback loop in improving your information-sharing policy and practice (1, 5)
- Keep up to date with new legislation and guidance impacting on information-sharing.

Sources

1   Department of Health (2013) *Information: To share or not to share? The Information Governance Review* (Caldicott2), Williams Lea for the Department of Health.
London: DH, https://www.gov.uk/government/uploads/system/uploads/attachment_data/file/192572/2900774_InfoGovernance_accv2.pdf (last accessed 21 December 2014).
2   The Centre of Excellence for Information Sharing (CEIS), http://information-sharing.co.uk (last accessed 21 December 2014).
3   Leicestershire Multi-Agency information-sharing hub, www.leics.gov.uk/index/mash (last accessed 21 December 2014).
4   Richardson, S. (2007) The challenge of inter-agency information sharing: a systemic study of two Sure Start children's centres, University of Plymouth PhD thesis.
5   Yang, T. and Maxwell, T. (2011) Information sharing in public organizations: a literature review of inter-personal, intra-organizational and inter-organizational success factors, *Government Information Quarterly* (US), 28: 164–75.
6   Office of the Information Commissioner, http://www.ico.org.uk. See particularly: data sharing page,
http://www.ico.org.uk/for_organisations/data_protection/topic_guides/data_sharing (last accessed 21 December 2014); Privacy impact assessment page,
http://www.ico.org.uk/for_organisations/data_protection/topic_guides/privacy_impact_assessment (last accessed 21 December 2014).

Conclusion

The chapter has given a brief overview of different theoretical approaches to information-sharing, focusing on systems approaches and on how using the ideas from the communities of practice approach can help in understanding the complexities in information-sharing.

Key concepts have been the interplay of reification and participation in communities of practice and the importance of understanding other professionals' practices of confidentiality for improving the quality of information-sharing.

Think points

- What would you say is your primary focus – a) individual services users, b) families, c) the wider community or the general public? If you think it is a mixture of two or more, which is dominant?
- Do you know the primary focus of those you might want to share information with or who might want to share it with you? Do you think this might affect how they might want or need to share information?
- Do you identify most strongly with your profession, your service, your team, your employer organization or another community of practice? (Some or all of these might be the same in your case but are not the same for everyone.) How do you think this might affect your practice of confidentiality and your understanding of the practices of confidentiality of the practitioners you work with?

Note: research for this chapter was supported by funding from the Economic and Social Research Council (studentship award number: PTA-030-2003-00162 and grant number: ES/K00557X/1).

11

Integrated approaches to special educational needs

Michael Cotton

Introduction

By utilizing historical perspectives towards the law relating to children it can be demonstrated that slow progress has been made towards accepting that all children's needs should be recognized and that they can be educated together. In the British context the Education Act 1944 declared that children should be educated according to age, ability and aptitude and outlined 11 categories of handicap, but the prevailing culture still ensured that children should fit schools, rather than schools adapt to children.

Some children were deemed 'uneducable' until the Education (Handicapped Children) Act 1970, which transferred the provision of training for 'mentally handicapped' children from health authorities to local education authorities (LEAs), so around 24,000 children in junior training centres and special care units, 8,000 in hospitals and an uncertain number at home or in private institutions ceased to be treated as 'mentally deficient' and became entitled to special education.

The government-commissioned Warnock Report (DES 1978) introduced the term 'special educational needs' (SEN) for the first time and brought 'handicapped children' into mainstream education. The underpinning research suggested up to 20 per cent of children may have SEN at some point in their school career. The subsequent Education Act 1981 defined SEN, made LEAs responsible for identification of SEN, and introduced statutory assessment and plans for them called statements of SEN. The Education Act 1993 established the first guidance for LEAs and their partners, the *SEN Code of Practice* and introduced the idea that every school should have a Special Educational Needs Coordinator (SENCo), with responsibility for helping colleagues to identify and make provision for those with SEN. It also launched a national SEN Tribunal to which families who were not happy with the provision could appeal. The Education

Act 1996, together with further amendments in the Special Education Needs & Disability Act 2001, proposed that children with SEN should be educated in mainstream schools unless it is incompatible with the provision of efficient education and/or the wishes of parents. In 2002 a revised SEN *Code of Practice* was published to reflect these changes and to offer guidance on how to implement them.

There has therefore been a national system for assessing and planning for children and young people with SEN since 1983, when the 1981 Act was implemented, leading to multi-disciplinary assessments of children and young people's educational needs and statements describing those needs and the additional provision that the LEA would make to meet those needs, sometimes with support from care or health services. It took 30 years for new legislation to make significant changes to this process. This chapter explores the nature of multi-professional work with children who have special needs and analyses contemporary shifts and developments.

Drivers for the proposed changes

Since the dawn of the twenty-first century there has been a plethora of commissioned reports on aspects of children's services with a health, care or education focus using similar language and coming to related recommendations and conclusions. In 2001 the Department of Health published a White Paper: *Valuing People – A New Strategy for Learning Disabilities for the 21st Century* (DoH 2001b) containing themes that have surfaced again and again in subsequent strategies, guidance, reports and finally in legislation in 2014. The government's primary objective then was to promote holistic services for people with learning disabilities through effective partnership working between all relevant local agencies in commissioning and delivery of services. Its sub-objectives included to ensure or enable that children and young people with learning disabilities:

- gain maximum life chance benefits from educational opportunities, health care and social care;
- have as much choice and control as possible over their lives through advocacy and a person-centred approach to planning the services they need, including over where, and how, they live;
- can access a health service designed around their individual needs;
- lead full and purposeful lives within their community and develop a range of friendships, activities and relationships;
- participate in all forms of employment, wherever possible in paid work and to make a valued contribution to the world of work.

The Valuing People Now movement has kept the faith and continued to promote these principles of person-centred planning in pockets of good practice across the country and, through lobbying by organizations such as the National Development Team for Inclusion, has finally seen these outcomes in legislation or statutory guidance in education, health and care. The 2004 SEN Strategy 'Removing Barriers to Achievement', which set out the government's vision on SEN, suggested to local authorities that 'the proportion of children educated in special schools should fall over time' and there should be a 'reduced reliance on statements'. Baroness Warnock, the architect of the original SEN legislation, reviewed its working in 2005 (Warnock 2005), and was concerned that a governmental overemphasis on inclusion in mainstream schools, following international trends, was encouraging local authorities to close special schools and causing anxiety to children and their families by 'forcing' them into mainstream schools where they were struggling with the demands made on them.

The House of Commons Education and Skills Committee in 2006 concluded that, 'the SEN system is demonstrably no longer fit for purpose and there is a need for the Government to develop a new system that puts the needs of the child at the centre of provision' (p. 10). It also recommended a radical review of the statutory assessment process. There was no ministerial will to do so at that point.

Subsequent reports about speech, language and communication needs (Bercow 2008); dyslexia and literacy difficulties (Rose 2009); parental confidence in the system of special education needs (Lamb 2009); and a report on teacher supply for those with profound and multiple learning difficulties (Salt 2010) each made specific recommendations but also came up with some broadly similar conclusions that joined up services, tailoring support around the needs of the children, a wide range of measurements for success, equipping the workforce and raising standards would improve the life chances of a range of children with SEN and disabilities.

As part of the reforms, following a number of reports about failings in the system to protect children, *Every Child Matters* (ECM) (DfES 2003) introduced a single set of five outcomes for all children and young people to achieve that applied to the work of all agencies and organizations working with children and young people. Being healthy, staying safe, enjoying and achieving, making a positive contribution and achieving economic well-being were agreed to be universal ambitions independent of background or circumstances. All agencies were expected to share information appropriately (a frequent issue in almost all safeguarding failures), and a system of common assessment for all members of the children's workforce was launched in 2004. Team-around-the-child (TAC) became a commonly used term for getting professionals together with the family, sharing information and planning collectively to meet the ECM outcomes, where levels of need were below statutory thresholds for education or care. Key working and the notion of a lead professional to act as coordinator for a Common Assessment Framework (CAF) plan, to be the main link for the family and to signpost them to other services was advanced by this practice.

A review of CAF was commissioned by the Local Authorities' Research Consortium and carried out by the National Foundation for Educational Research (NFER) in 2011 (George et al. 2011). The report concluded that intervening early and in a coordinated fashion led to better outcomes that were achieved at lower cost than if they had been left or ignored until children became young people with poor health and lower educational attainment, invoking child protection or youth justice procedures. In general the CAF was seen to be cost effective in terms of preventing future failure at greater cost to society and reflects the conclusions of the Allen Report on early intervention described later.

One of the developments of the common assessment TAC approach was that the focus often moved from the 'child with the problem' to the 'family who need joined up support'. A Team-around-the-family (TAF) approach and the later Troubled Families Programme in 2011 have encouraged local authorities and their partners to consider reframing service design and delivery to achieve better outcomes more cost effectively; there are some examples of this in practice below.

A further initiative from the ECM programme was to establish a Children's Workforce Development Council in 2005 (closed in 2012 and replaced by the Teaching Agency) whose aim was to devise and implement a One Children's Workforce Framework for every professional working with children and young people from whatever agency. It attempted to create a shared identity, purpose, vision, values and a common language; integrated working practices; common elements of training for the entire workforce; and a focus on positive outcomes for children and young people. Its lasting legacy has been the raising of the status of early years professionals and some parts of the common language and practice appearing in job descriptions across the workforce, but the jury is out on how far the identity and vision have been absorbed by all those working with children and young people.

In other related fields, the Allen Report (Allen 2011) concluded that early intervention is 'the best sustainable structural deficit programme available' and went on to make a series of recommendations designed to improve the coherence of assessments for children under 5 between health and education services. The Munro Review (2011c) reviewed child protection and one of many recommendations was a focus on effective multi-agency working that allowed more freedom for professionals to use their expertise in assessing need and providing the right help. Among the government's responses to Professor Munro's report was that: 'Building a system centred on children and young people also means building even stronger partnerships between government, local authority children's services, the voluntary and community sector, social workers, education, the police and health services' (DfE 2011b: 5).

While the emphasis in this response is clearly on safeguarding children and young people and, in the Allen Report, on early intervention to improve social and emotional development, the sentiments expressed in both are consistent with the themes of being child-centred and outcome-led with integrated delivery, processes, strategy and governance; ideas which were first expressed in relation to the establishment of Children's Trusts in 2006.

Within health services, the Kennedy Review (DoH 2010), *Getting it Right for Children and Young People – Overcoming Cultural Barriers in the NHS*, pointed out how frustrated children and families become by the lack of coordination of services within health, for example multiple appointments in different locations on near-consecutive days and the lack of join-up or information-sharing, especially with education services.

Meanwhile, in education the most effective changes to the system for those with SEN from 1981 to 2001 included:

- a recognition of SEN throughout local authority and health services;
- an assumption of mainstream education and therefore a reduction in segregating children;
- assessment, planning and tracking progress of all children has improved;
- SEN support has increased, with clear guidance in an SEN *Code of Practice*;
- there are appeal processes for families if they are not happy with what they have been offered.

Nevertheless, as various reports have concluded, the system was no longer 'fit for purpose' as it stood and so in 2011 the British coalition government published a Green Paper for consultation, *Support and Aspiration: a new approach to special educational needs and disability* (DfE 2011c). This was a joint paper between the Department for Education (DfE) and the Department of Health (DH), thus reflecting a multi-disciplinary underpinning, and outlined the reasons for change as:

- too many children with SEN have their needs picked up late, and schools and colleges can focus too much on the SEN label rather than meeting the child's needs;
- the current Statements of SEN, or Learning Difficulty Assessments for those who have left school but still have SEN do not focus on life outcomes;
- too many families have to battle to find out what support is available and to get the help they need from education, health and social care services;
- young people with SEN do less well than their peers at school and college and are more likely to be out of education, training and employment at 18;
- when a young person leaves school for further education, they lose many of the rights and protections that exist in the SEN system in schools.

The vision in the consultation paper was certainly aspirational, mostly welcomed by professionals and parental organizations and was one of the mostly widely responded to consultations in education history. In 2012 a response to the consultation was published; *Progress and Next Steps* (DfE 2012) introduced the forthcoming legislation and suggested ways to test the reforms before finalizing the law. After a bidding process, 20 Pathfinders involving 31 local authorities and their health partners were set up across England and a number of voluntary sector partners were appointed to support aspects of the reforms.

What has changed?

The Children and Families Act 2014, and its accompanying guidance, the *Special Educational Needs and Disability (SEND) Code of Practice: 0–25 Years* (DfE/ DoH 2015), helped to transform thinking and practice about assessing and planning for children and young people with SEN and, for the first time, included children with disabilities.

The most significant process changes were as follows:

- to transfer all children and young people with Statements of SEN or Learning Difficulty Assessments to education, health and care plans;
- for a single system to run from birth to 25 years, giving the same statutory rights to all;
- to emphasize the preparation of young people for adulthood, that is for employment, living independently, making friends and relationships, belonging to their local communities and being healthy;
- for every local authority to publish a local offer of all services available to children up to 16 years, and young people up to 25 years and their families, from universal through targeted to specialist services;
- to offer a personal budget to young people and their families so they can make some choices, and have more control over the provision to support them.

In response to the Allen Report, the government made over £2 billion available to local authorities for early help services and set out parameters for good assessment of children and young people that included timeliness, the quality of assessment and the effectiveness of the help offered via locally agreed frameworks that were clearly understood by all partners. Some of this was echoed in revised guidance to professionals from the recommendations of the Munro Report. *Working Together to Safeguard Children* (DfE 2015) recommended that assessment should be child centred, holistic, informed by evidence, focused on actions and outcomes, involve children young people and their families and build on their strengths, all through an integrated approach. In a very similar and encouraging vein the SEND *Code of Practice* stated that education, health and care assessments must be person-centred and outcome-focused, involve close collaboration between education, health and care services and include children, young people and their parents in decision-making.

In specific relation to multi-professional working, a whole chapter of the SEND *Code of Practice* is devoted to 'Working together across education, health and care for joint outcomes' (see Chapter 3). There is a statutory duty on local authorities and their partners to develop joint commissioning arrangements to improve outcomes for all children with SEN and disabilities.

Some of the recommendations in the Kennedy report were incorporated into aspects of the Health and Social Care Act 2012, the NHS *Mandate* (DoH 2012a) from government to the NHS Commissioning Board and in the report on *Improving Children's and Young People's Health Outcomes* (DoH 2013). Of most relevance in this context is a framework for greater integration between the NHS and local government through the creation of local Health and Wellbeing Boards, which were intended to make Children's Trust Boards largely redundant. However, getting the Health and Wellbeing Boards to make children's services a priority for discussion and planning has proved difficult, so many local authorities have retained Children's Trust Boards to make sure that children's issues get an airing among chief officers. Clinical commissioning groups (CCGs), as local budget holders for health, are expected to work with local authorities to:

- jointly commission services for children at strategic or individual child levels;
- consider pooling budgets, or at least aligning some of them;
- share assessments;
- contribute to a local offer about their provision of services to children.

The NHS *Mandate* exhorts the health services to 'support children and young people with special educational needs and disabilities to ensure that (they) have access to services identified in their Care Plan . . . and that their parents are able to ask for a personal budget based on a single assessment across health, social care and education' (p. 5).

The Children and Young People's Health Outcomes Forum recommended that the NHS Commissioning Board should prioritize and promote integrated care provision. The response (DoH 2012) acknowledged that its focus had been more on structure and processes rather than on the views and experiences of children, young people and their families. It accepted that integration with education and social care 'requires working with other services and across government to lead to person-centred children's services' (para. 5.6).

Updated guidance was issued to local authorities and their partners in 2014, as the Children and Families Act amended part of the Children Act 1989, specifically Section 22 to promote the education of looked-after children. The guidance acknowledged that the majority of children in care have SEN and exhorts professionals to consider how care plans complement EHC plans to tell a 'coherent and comprehensive story of how children's needs are being met' (para. 29) and to avoid unnecessary duplication of information. This resonates well with the 'Tell Us Once' approach of the SEND *Code of Practice* as a way of streamlining the processes for families and professionals.

A related piece of legislation followed the Children and Families Act through the legislative process resulting in the Care Act 2014 which also requires local authorities to work to promote the integration of adult care and support with health services. Around the point of transition from children's services to adult care services the language of the two Acts is the same and there is an overlap of responsibilities described in the Acts that should ensure no young person falls through a gap between services.

The SEND *Code of Practice* is equally clear that 'the local authority **must** [a legal requirement, not just "it would be good if . . ."] engage other partners it thinks appropriate to support children and young people' (with SEND). It goes on to list those that might be considered, including private, voluntary and community sector organizations, child and adolescent mental health services (CAMHS), local therapists, Jobcentre Plus and their employment support advisers, training, apprenticeship and supported employment providers, housing associations, leisure and play services.

In order to improve services and outcomes and to be responsive to local needs, local authorities and CCGs *must* also engage with local Healthwatch organizations, patient groups, parent and carer forums, groups representing young people, and other local voluntary and community organizations.

The rhetoric is clear in the legislation: whether it is education, care or health based, local authorities and their partners in health must plan and commission together and consider integrated provision and pooled budgets. How far has this translated into practice?

Practice examples

The contrast between trying to mould people into existing services rather than construct a package of care around them is nicely illustrated by an example from the Voluntary Organisations' Disability Group (*Guardian* July 2011). Joe was a teenager with learning disabilities and autism, sectioned under the Mental Health Act, eating only crisps and physically restrained up to 15 times a day. A charity stepped in, worked with the local authority and a multi-professional team, built up trust with Joe, and together they created a bespoke care package so that he is now living semi-independently in a house with friends.

Since the advent of SEND Pathfinders trialling aspects of the intended Children and Families Act legislation, there are increasing examples of good practice. Much emphasis has been placed on the importance of co-production with families and young people, sitting down with a blank sheet of paper and designing things together, rather than the clichéd 'consultation with', whereby statutory agencies go out to tell families what they intend to do and ask if there are any questions. This has brought parents, carers and young people into decision-making and strategic planning forums, often for the first time in local authorities. In local authority areas, there are examples of local parent carer forums' involvement with the local authority and its partners in planning and implementing the reforms, such as designing a format for an education, health and care plan and agreeing the content and design for a local offer (Mott MacDonald 2015). In North Yorkshire, for example, a group of disabled young people, when asked their opinion of the developing local offer on the local authority website declared it boring and unreadable, resulting in the creation of a young people's version on the youth support service website, with a focus on preparing for adulthood. In Newcastle, the parent and carer forum has worked with the local authority to promote personal transport budgets through 'Pass It On Parents'. The city council has also commissioned a local user-led voluntary organization for disabled people to develop and write a guide to personal budgets: *The Big Handbook*.

An increasing number of local authorities have taken the opportunity, at least partly prompted by the legislation, to reconsider their service design. Examples include: moving from providing services for only 0–19 years to making continuous provision from 0–25 years, for example in Portsmouth; combining SEN and disability services, such as in North Yorkshire; therapeutic health services managed within the local authority, as in Barnsley; and a combined education, health and care service, managed at arm's length by an independent contractor in Devon. These show some of the variety of configurations now being developed and tried.

In terms of personalization, at a national-level Think Local, Act Personal (TLAP) is a national partnership, chaired by the Association of Directors of Adult Social Services (ADASS), with more than 50 member organizations spanning central and local government, the NHS, the provider sector, people with care and support needs, carers and family members. Participants are committed to transforming health and care through personalization and community-based support. In a similar vein, the Coalition for Collaborative Care (C4CC) brings together people with long-term conditions and organizations from across the health, social care and voluntary sectors that believe people should be in charge of their own lives. Individuals with long-term conditions have their own unique experience, knowledge and skills and should be the main decision-makers about designing their support and managing their conditions.

At an individual level, the websites for Preparing for Adulthood, In-Control and Kids each have examples, respectively, of: person-centred planning where imagination, determination and coordination of effort have demonstrably improved life outcomes for young adults and their families; the use of resource allocation systems to indicate personal budgets and how this has given more choice and control over provision of services to young people; and how some families have used personal budgets in imaginative ways to meet the needs of their disabled child. All of these require different ways of thinking about how services are provided and will only be successful when local organizations, including the voluntary and community sectors, work together with young people and their families.

Research findings

The Local Government Research Group commissioned NFER to research several aspects of the reforms (George et al. 2011). In 2011, they undertook a small sample, in-depth survey of local authority perceptions of the Green Paper *Support and Aspiration*. The main conclusions were that local authorities welcomed proposals for greater partnership with the voluntary and community sectors (VCS), and they accepted the need for better integration, commissioning and accountability across agencies. Most thought that they were already integrating some services and, interestingly, they perceived that working collaboratively to complete EHC plans would put more demands on agencies and lengthen the process – the opposite of what the proposals were intended to achieve. The DfE have done a series of implementation surveys of local authorities and their partners and triangulated these with questioning local parent-carer forums. Among the headline results of the 2015 survey, the percentage of local authorities who were extremely or very confident that their EHC assessments and plans would be completed within the 20-week statutory timetable has decreased from 59 per cent in February to 36 per cent in June 2015. Working collaboratively may be a small part of the problems of timeliness, but more of this is likely to be related to the relative newness of the processes, such that practice is not yet embedded and also to the pressure on capacity among all professionals, particularly within local authorities under financial and consequently staffing pressures.

Transition from school to adulthood has often been an unsatisfactory or unsuccessful experience for young people with SEN. They are over-represented in the 'not in education, employment or training' (NEET) figures and they often leave school less prepared for and without support for whatever ambitions they want to achieve. This is documented in another report commissioned by the Local Government Research Group from Sloper et al. (2011). They suggested that hope for the future came in a number of initiatives such as person-centred planning, multi-agency transition panels and teams, transition champions and development work with schools and families. Some authorities have adopted these service arrangements and all should now be using person-centred planning as the basis for creating plans for any individual's future. Better news from the DfE summer survey (see above) was that more than 95 per cent of practitioners in local authorities felt they were doing at least 'quite well or better' in ensuring that families' experiences were at the centre of any reviews of their child.

Despite the Department of Health's intentions about good practice in moving from children's to adults' services since 2008, a Care Quality Commission (CQC) report in 2014 concluded that families are still confused about the next steps and the coordination of help for their young people. The report found some examples of good practice where the common factors were: consistent staff who knew the young person, with a key person involved in any handovers; adolescent clinics dealing with 10–19-year-olds; good communication with families and between professionals; and good quality information about next steps. NHS England is coordinating a nationwide initiative to get local health commissioners and providers to develop transition protocols (Cornish 2015). Some are involving their local authority colleagues appropriately but there is a good argument to say that the focus is wrongly placed on internal NHS processes and not on what matters to young people as they get older, who just want to ensure that their care will continue without interruption when they reach 18 years old.

SQW is a research organization commissioned by the Department for Education to report on the progress made by SEND Pathfinders and on specific aspects of the reforms nationally. One of a number of thematic reports produced in 2014 was about the relationship between education and care in implementing the reforms (Spivack et al. 2014). SQW found some examples of existing good practice and several changes prompted by the impending legislation of structural reform, creating a variety of multi-agency services; some small scale examples of joint commissioning; and a few occasions where social care staff were directly involved in SEND Pathfinder developments, delivery and multi-agency training.

A second thematic report (Craston et al. 2014) on collaboration between local authorities and health demonstrated that Pathfinder status led to the strategic involvement of health in governance, consideration of joint commissioning or at least some integrated resourcing. This is not surprising as they were requirements of successful bidding to be a Pathfinder. Positive spin-offs came in the form of starting to share values, understand working cultures, improve relationships, training together and in some cases creating multi-disciplinary and or co-located teams. This latter development, although welcomed, had created challenges which had not been fully addressed by the time of the research and that will be discussed in the next section.

Within education, the SQW research reports (Hill et al. 2014) found some examples of schools involved with the local authority and parent/carers in developing and piloting aspects of EHC planning, key working and contributing to the local offer. Local authorities have a relatively new relationship with further education (FE) and the demands on the post-school sector to work with the local authority are very new (Thom et al. 2014). Some local authorities were successfully developing engagement through, for example, FE SEND Networks, mirroring those for schools. Relationships were, understandably, noted to be stronger with general FE colleges and sixth forms and more sensitive with specialist independent sector providers (ISPs) who are feeling somewhat threatened by funding reforms, EHC planning expectations and a move in many local authorities to develop or improve local provision, rather than send young people to out-of-authority placements.

The SQW evaluation on the impact of the first 18 months of Pathfinder activity (Craston et al. 2013a) showed evidence of better joint working with families and between professionals, on behalf of families involved in the trials. The report on the process and implementation (Craston et al. 2013b) suggested that progress had been made in training professionals to understand the culture change needed to put children, young people and their families at the heart of the process. They found examples of professionals collaborating and sharing at planning meetings and better sharing of information between agencies and with families. All of this is an encouraging endorsement of the intended reforms.

What is of paramount importance in all these reforms is that outcomes for children and young people enhance their life chances, through effective multi-professional working. The University of Lancaster, in conjunction with In-Control, a national charity working for an inclusive society 'where everyone has the support they need to live a good life and make a valued contribution' (from the In-Control website), were commissioned by the Department for Education to create and trial a Personal Outcomes Evaluation Tool (POET) for children and young people. There was previously a version of POET surveying perceptions of individual planning and budgeting in adult care services. The children's version had two trial phases in volunteer local authorities by the end of 2014 and an interim report was published in 2015 (Waters et al. 2015), before a third trial and a final revision planned for later that year. Initial conclusions were that around half the families who responded valued the professional support in planning and valued the partnership towards agreed outcomes for their child. Generally they were positive about the flexibility of the new processes and thought it gave them some more control and choice. Almost all the professionals felt it improved their relationship with families, but views were very mixed about whether it improved multi-agency working, communication or decision-making across a range of professionals (only 40 per cent agreed). Common concerns from parents and professionals were about timeliness of the assessment process and the paperwork involved. Both of these are to be expected at this stage in implementing new and complex procedures until the processes are better understood and more firmly embedded in practice.

What are the remaining challenges?

One of the most significant aspirations in the Green Paper *Support and Aspiration* has not made it through the legislative process: the single assessment and plan for children with SEND that would have accompanied them through their lives to adulthood. One child, one plan encompassing their education, health and social care needs with achievable outcomes agreed by all the statutory agencies proved to be a legislative step too far, requiring changes to primary legislation in health and social care that ministers were unwilling to contemplate at a time when health services were undergoing massive reorganization. This is disappointing when, during the same period, new legislation for adult services was being drafted, the processes for social work assessment and planning for children in need were being reviewed, and early help services were being redefined. Despite the view that families should 'tell us once' and professionals would then share the relevant information with those for whom it is appropriate, having different legislative requirements in each of the statutory agencies means that professionals will continue to ask and families will still have to tell their stories more often than they should need to.

Some hope emerges from experimentation in social care services to be more flexible in the assessment process and timescales following from the Munro Review (2011c). The government issued formal directions to eight local authorities in 2011 to test a more flexible approach – the impact of which was reviewed by the Childhood Wellbeing Research Centre (Munro and Lushey 2012). A small number of professionals working in partner agencies were interviewed and were positive about streamlining assessments, having clearer formats for planning and for agency roles. Disappointingly there were concerns about whether the reforms were sustainable after the trial period. Some local authorites, such as County Durham (Durham County Council 2014), have adopted the practice fully by replacing the common assessment and child-in-need assessments, and have introduced an early help assessment, a team around the family meeting to plan a full care assessment only where the lower level assessment is not deemed sufficient. While this remains a care assessment procedure, the process has removed initial and core assessments, has shortened timescales and eradicated repetition. There is evidence that the Children and Families Act is beginning to improve practice and as a result authorities are asking families and professionals only for information that is new and different from that already held.

A recurring theme in the SQW research reports picked up from Pathfinders, and recognized latterly by the Departments of Education and Health, has been the culture changes required by legislation and its accompanying guidance, and an acknowledgement that this takes time to embed. Making people change the way they act, through compliance with legislation for example, should begin to make them change the way they think; it is one of the bases for cognitive behavioural therapy, after all. However, altering practice for reasons of compliance is a slow way to change thinking and feeling. In order for such culture change to be successful, young people, their families and the professionals involved in supporting them have to believe it is making a real difference to people's lives, and that takes longer to achieve than changing the paperwork.

Other challenges identified and reported in research findings (Craston et al. 2013a, 2013b) that are relevant to improving multi-professional teamwork include those of sharing information between different IT systems and between those with different working cultures, and reducing the duplication of assessments and plans. *Working Together* guidance suggested that local authorities and their partners should develop and publish local protocols for assessment that would, among other things, clarify how statutory assessments will be informed by other specialist assessments, for example those for SEND. It would ensure that such assessments are coordinated so that children and families experience a joined-up assessment and a single planning process focused on outcomes. Many local authorities have considered how review meetings for children in care with

SEN can be brought together at least once a year so that one of the personal education plan reviews and an annual review of the EHC plan can be done on the same day if not actually during the same meeting. This is a small step but at least in the right direction.

In working with health colleagues the challenges are perhaps greater. Administrative boundaries are not necessarily coterminous with local authority borders and governance is very different. Thinking about patients, diagnosis and treatment puts the medical model at odds with a social model of disability where planning is based on supporting people to achieve outcomes that they have chosen, rather than on a prescribed treatment plan. NHS England is working with Clinical Commissioning Groups and training designated medical officers; many local authorities have been arranging joint training with their health colleagues to share the language and thinking behind the reforms, but culture change is hard, as was discussed earlier.

Could or should multi-professional teamworking include or involve the VCS? Increasingly, as local government budgets are squeezed, authorities are becoming commissioners of services rather than providers. One of the main strands of the legislative changes and guidance is that of personalization and people taking more control over their own lives. The publication of a local offer by every local authority, the offer of personal budgets to those with a statutory plan and the shared decision-making with families and young people all help to promote choice and control. VCS organizations are being commissioned, at strategic levels or for individuals, to provide services that families have chosen to support them to achieve the outcomes which the local authority has agreed to write into a plan and that are not within the power or control of the authority to offer. Thus VCS staff will more frequently be part of multi-professional teams at reviews and adding to assessments in future.

Conclusion

In conclusion, this chapter has argued that some of the previous architecture intended to integrate children's services was dismantled following the 2010 general election: Every Child Matters, Children's Trust Boards, Sure Start, the Children's Workforce Development Council and its national competency framework, and Contact Point which would have registered every single child on a national database.

Multi-disciplinary working in services for children with SEND is enshrined in legislation in the NHS Act 2006, the Health and Social Care Act 2012, the Children and Families Act 2014 and the Care Act 2014. It is also promoted in health guidance through the NHS Mandate 2012, care guidance, in *Working Together to Safeguard Children* (revised 2015) and in education through the SEND *Code of Practice* 2015.

There are examples of effective but isolated multi-disciplinary practice, some due to deliberate structural change, some because of money-saving co-location and some due to relationships forming between front-line workers working with children and young people.

Culture change to achieve personalization of services to enable people to become more independent takes time and requires leaders who understand and promote it and who are not afraid of structural reorganization, of joint commissioning, of pooling budgets to reach similar ends, and of giving up what they have been offering because it is not what people want from statutory services.

Personalization of services, adapting what we do to meet families' needs, developing new partnerships and looking outside of local authority/CCG services to offer real choice and control is a huge challenge to thinking and practice but is more satisfying for professionals, requires them to think with imagination and is more likely to satisfy families and help their children to achieve good life outcomes.

A national accountability framework and Ofsted/CQC inspection of local area SEND services from 2016 will focus minds on how well we are doing to make lives better for children and young people with SEN and disabilities no matter who we work for.

Think points

- The Localism Act 2010 gave new rights and powers to local communities to ensure that 'local social enterprises, volunteers and community groups with a bright idea for improving local services get a chance to change how things are done'. In what ways might local groups or communities be encouraged to drive improvements in provision and services for children and young people with SEND?
- A high proportion of children in care have SEN. The primary legislation is unlikely to change again soon so how might the guidance governing assessment and planning for children in care and that for children with SEND be brought together so that children, young people and their families have fewer assessments, reviews and separate plans?
- If culture change is one of the most important but also more intractable or slowly developing areas of development, what ideas do you have for how multi-professional teams can understand each other's language and ways of working, and how to accommodate different governance arrangements in order to achieve the same goals for the benefit of the lives of children and their families?

12

Multi-agency working to safeguard children from child sexual exploitation

Paul Hill

Introduction

This chapter reflects on multi-disciplinary policy and practice for safeguarding children from child sexual exploitation (CSE) and also describes the arrangements that have been put in place to enquire into allegations of historic CSE. The chapter argues that multi-professional responses that go beyond the traditional child welfare professional community are essential in underpinning the challenge to the sexual exploitation of children and young people. The chapter explores a range of issues – from prevention through to prosecution – which together provide a comprehensive, partnership approach to CSE.

The English national context

Professional and public awareness of CSE has grown significantly in the years since the publication of the first dedicated national guidance for dealing with this form of child sexual abuse, which was significantly entitled *Safeguarding Children Involved in Prostitution* (DoH 2000). Changes in legislation, guidance and attitudes culminated in the publication of the national *Tackling Child Sexual Exploitation: Action Plan* (DfE 2011a). This conceptual shift from 'child prostitution' to 'child sexual exploitation' is highly significant in aiding our understanding of CSE. The utilization of the concept 'child prostitution' led to policy and practice which spoke of the 'lifestyle choices of the young people' and 'young people enjoying the rewards of the lifestyle'. Young people were seen as 'prostitutes' rather than victims, and abusers were seen as 'punters' rather than criminals. The shift towards the utilization of the concept CSE which took place around 2005 led to significant developments in policy and practice and contributed to the growth of multi-professional practice approaches.

A growing appreciation of the need to develop a more sophisticated multi-agency response to CSE was aided by a number of factors including the two-year national inquiry into CSE by 'gangs and groups' led by Sue Berelowitz, then the deputy children's commissioner for England (Office of the Children's Commissioner for England 2012–13). A further significant landmark was the publication of *The Independent Inquiry into Child Sexual Exploitation in Rotherham 1997– 2013* (known as the 'The Jay Report', Rotherham MBC 2014), which emphasized the importance of strong strategic and political leadership across the public sector and in communities in responding to CSE at a local level.

As a result of the publication of the Jay Report the national inspectorate Ofsted announced that it would be undertaking inspections of local responses to CSE practice and policy in eight local authority areas. The Ofsted report, *Thematic Inspection* (2014) considered evidence from 36 inspections of children's services that had already been published and inspections of 38 children's homes, in addition to the eight specific CSE inspections. This detailed report has produced 25 recommendations for local authorities, partner organizations, Local Safeguarding Children Boards (LSCBs), national government and Ofsted itself. Overarching themes in the findings and recommendations include: the need for strong strategic leadership; the need to develop effective local performance arrangements (informed by consistent crime recording); the need to prioritize awareness-raising; the importance of police and local authorities using all powers to disrupt and prosecute offenders; and the need to ensure that all missing children have an independent return interview and that intelligence about missing episodes is collated to identify patterns and risks. While the report does emphasize the importance of effective multi-agency working, particularly when presenting findings about professional practice, the focus of comments about strategic leadership is entirely on the local authority and the LSCB. Therefore the distinctive strategic leadership that can be offered by the police service or by health trusts and commissioners in developing therapeutic services is not fully explored. It can be argued that the report does not provide sufficient analysis of the examples of good practice identified in some areas. As a consequence, it has been argued that an opportunity to promote good practice has been missed.

The Ofsted report is of assistance in developing understanding of the complexity of CSE and of the necessity to develop a sophisticated 'whole system', multi-agency response to this form of abuse. It is possible to benchmark planning and activity against some good practice identified in the report. Partnership working to address CSE in the local authority area considered in this chapter dates from 1995. Reflecting on developments since then during 2011 the independent chair of the LSCB sought assurance as to the effectiveness of the multi-agency response to CSE. In common with other organizations nationally, it is recognized that the police and the council did not have the same rigorous and coordinated approach to dealing with allegations of CSE that has subsequently been developed.

A multi-agency response to CSE

The shift from 'child prostitution' as an organizing idea towards 'child sexual exploitation' has facilitated more effective multi-professional responses. The author of this chapter has been involved in a number of initiatives including:

- appointing a 'Champion against CSE': a police superintendent;
- developing a multi-agency co-located service, known as the 'Hub';
- the LSCB being responsible for the strategic response to CSE;
- the director of children's services (DCS) convening a meeting for all secondary headteachers to discuss CSE;
- the council's strategic leadership team devoting an extended meeting to the topic of CSE, receiving a detailed presentation from LSCB (Local Safeguarding Children Board) setting out the current incidence of CSE, the deployment of services, the current challenges and new developments in partnership working.

The full partnership approach to opposing CSE is embodied in the 'Hub' – a co-located multi-professional setting. The organizations co-located in the Hub include children's services, voluntary organizations, an NHS district care trust and the police, with other partner organizations being linked.

After one year of practice a review of the operation of the Hub was undertaken. The review considered a number of sources of information including:

- operational data provided by the Hub;
- CSE case file audits undertaken by managers from the police and children's social services;
- a university research project into the experiences of young people affected by CSE, facilitated by the voluntary sector and supported by the British Association for the Study and Prevention of Child Abuse and Neglect (BASPCAN);
- a self-assessment of CSE partnership working against standards developed by the University of Bedfordshire;
- a Home Office Innovation Fund evaluation of parental support work undertaken by Parents Against Child Exploitation (PACE);
- information from external scrutiny of the Hub by Ofsted and the National College of Policing.

Key members of the LSCB and the independent chair presented the findings of this review to the council chief executive and the DCS in order to take the multi-professional partnership to the next level of development. Key issues identified by the review included:

- Since the Hub was established operational pressures had resulted in increased dedicated staffing resources from both children's social care services and the police. Increases in staffing had been primarily aimed at enhancing management and administrative capacity.

- Audit of practice showed that cases were generally well managed within the Hub. The presence of a social work team manager in the Hub strengthened joint working between the police and social workers. Revised referral pathways for CSE cases were implemented as a result of learning from audit.

- The Hub had now been externally scrutinized by both Ofsted (as part of the 2014 inspection of local authority children's services) and the National College of Policing. Ofsted (2014) found that: 'The co-location of police, social care and Barnardo's within the CSE Hub is a particular strength. It promotes effective and early information sharing across agencies where children and young people are at risk of or are suffering sexual exploitation. Timely and robust multi-agency involvement ensures that risks of CSE are identified and plans put in place to reduce these risks.' The National College of Policing awarded the Hub 'Gold Standard' and has encouraged other police forces to adopt this operational approach as best practice.

- The review concluded that, working with the Hub model, partners had shown themselves responsive to increasing demand and complexity of cases and working arrangements. The review noted that it is likely that demand will continue to increase, at least in the medium term.

Having learnt from the review and following the publication of the Jay Report in 2014, the council's strategic leadership team devoted most of a regular meeting to considering the lessons and considering the implications. A briefing for all elected members was prepared and circulated on behalf of the DCS. The strategic leadership team's considerations resulted in the drafting of a motion regarding CSE which was unanimously passed by the council. Achieving political engagement around CSE is a key element of a partnership approach. The LSCB has delivered specific training sessions for elected members regarding CSE. Materials have been developed which enable every member of the council to undertake training about CSE: this course is delivered in a manner that is accessible to elected members, and addresses the incidence and signs of CSE. It provides opportunities for elected members to undertake further reading and describes the processes for getting help for children and families in the district. It also focuses on the specific roles of elected members in terms of safeguarding and CSE, and the course is continuing professional development certificated.

Preventative services

As well as responding to the current and historic cases of CSE it is also essential that there is a multi-professional approach to prevention. Services have been commissioned from voluntary and community sector partners which led to a programme which included:

- every year 10 students attending a CSE-based drama performed by a theatre in education company which is reinforced by pre- and post-performance lesson plans for schools to deliver;
- work in one locality being boosted to provide more preventative group work for young people and to train peer mentors;
- a voluntary organization being commissioned to expand its work to support more boys and young men, and to develop a new resource pack for work with families to raise awareness of CSE; this resource pack will be evaluated by a local university;
- PACE (Parents Against Child Exploitation) being commissioned to provide intensive support to the parents of children who are known to be experiencing CSE, and to train local practitioners to deliver specific support materials developed by PACE to parents and carers whose children may be at risk from CSE.

Additional preventative work was later also developed to include:

- exploring options for developing more accessible sources of advice and assistance for black and minority ethnic women;
- work with the youth service to develop artwork, 'consequences cards' and accessible online- and social media-based advice for young people;
- work with faith and community groups to raise awareness of CSE, to have honest conversations about the incidence, patterns and impact of CSE and ensuring that local people understand how they can identify and report CSE;
- work with the city solicitor, licensing and environmental health colleagues to ensure that the full range of regulatory powers are utilized by the council to ensure that the local area is a 'hostile environment' for those considering abusing children and young people; CSE training is being provided for staff in these services.

This adds up to a comprehensive preventative package in relation to CSE.

Practice experience and research demonstrate that children are sometimes transported, or 'trafficked' for the purposes of CSE. The police have had some successes in preventing children being trafficked in private cars and there is evidence that some perpetrators are making use of public transport as a potentially less risky means of trafficking children. It is recognized that public transport providers and the British Transport Police are increasingly vigilant regarding this issue.

An important strand of preventative work is engaging with communities and leaders to raise awareness of CSE. Across the relevant sub-region, LSCBs and the police have developed a 'Know the Signs' campaign which provides clear messages about CSE in the form of posters for public spaces, schools and other settings, small information cards for children, parents and professionals, and a range of internet-based awareness-raising tools.

In addition, the LSCB and children's services developed a partnership with the local Council for Mosques and a Muslim association to support mosques and madrasas throughout the district to deliver good safeguarding children arrangements. This provided opportunities to deliver key messages about a range of safeguarding issues, including CSE, in training events for staff and volunteers and in meetings with parents. In addition, the LSCB is supporting some groups who have expressed an interest in developing community-based CSE campaigns and services.

Heightened interest in this issue, following the publication of the Jay Report, has resulted in invitations to the LSCB, the council and the police to speak at public meetings about the issue of CSE.

In addition to responding to requests to speak at community-organized events it is important that the council and its partners continue to create opportunities to broadcast key messages about CSE and safeguarding children to all communities in the local area. It is important that the local authorities makes use of structures and community fora to ensure that there is a positive dialogue about CSE across the whole area. It is for this reason that local authorities should use their local political and community engagement structures to receive a report and stimulate discussion about CSE.

In any communication with the public regarding CSE it is important to ensure the issue is understood in the wider context of child abuse and neglect, in particular child sexual abuse. If parents, carers and wider communities are to effectively prevent CSE and protect children from CSE it is necessary that agencies make it clear that there are a number of models of CSE and grooming, the most prominent of which are:

- Peer-on-peer exploitation: children are sexually exploited by peers who are known to them at school, in the neighbourhood or through mutual friends.

- Exploitation through befriending and grooming: children are befriended directly by the perpetrator or through other children and young people. This process may begin with a girl or boy being targeted and befriended by a young boy or girl usually known to them as an equal, i.e. a classmate, a friend of a sibling, or a neighbour.

- The 'boyfriend'/pimp model of exploitation: perpetrators target children posing as 'boyfriends', showering the child with attention and gifts to cause infatuation. They initiate a sexual relationship with the child, which the child is expected to return as 'proof' of her/his love or as a way of returning the initial attention and gifts. The child is effectively told that they owe the perpetrators money for cigarettes, alcohol, drugs and car rides and that sexual activities are one way of paying it back.

- The 'party' model: parties are organized by groups of adults to lure young people. Young people are offered drinks, drugs and car rides, often for free. They are introduced to an exciting environment and a culture where sexual promiscuity and violence are normalized. Parties are held at various locations and children are persuaded (sometimes financially) to bring their peers along.

It is recognized that in some instances CSE is an activity deliberately embarked upon by a pre-existing gang, in part for the purpose of extending the control and influence of the gang among young people in the community. This model of abuse was the subject of extensive research by the Office of the Children's Commissioner. In other instances groups of adults, who are otherwise unconnected, network and operate together solely for the purpose of targeting, grooming and abusing children through CSE. Each of the models described above can be implemented either face to face, through so-called 'street grooming', or the perpetrators can make use of the internet and social media to target and groom the victim. A risk of focusing on one particular model of CSE, or on 'street grooming' rather than online grooming is that parents or carers may fail to recognize the signs that a child is at risk. In addition, a focus on one model can lead to assumptions about the characteristics of perpetrators, for example in terms of ethnicity or age, which may make it easier for abusers not conforming to a particular stereotype to harm children. Multi-agency cooperation is required to address each of these models.

Strategic responses

For multi-agency working to be effective it should be underpinned by a coherent strategic approach. In the local area considered in this case study developments have been guided by a nine point strategic response to CSE. This contains the following key points:

- the partnership response to CSE is child, young person and victim focused;
- a multi-agency co-located team will work together to reduce the risk to victims and bring offenders to justice;
- a bespoke training plan will be developed for all professionals and particularly for schools to identify to pupils and teachers the signs of being groomed for CSE;
- a plan will be developed for all faith and community leaders to support communities through the damage caused by CSE;

- a support network will be developed focusing on women and mothers;
- a specific direct work plan will be developed aimed at boys between 14 and 17 years to tackle any unacceptable attitudes regarding the sexual abuse of any person;
- a specific product will be developed for the Pakistani origin community which addresses child sexual exploitation and explores the harm that this offence can cause to individuals and communities;
- a partnership response will be developed to reduce the opportunities for perpetrators of CSE to traffic and abuse children and young people through the use of all regulatory functions of the council and its partners;
- the multi-professional partnership response includes undertaking multi-agency historic investigations into CSE.

The CSE sub-group of the LSCB is responsible for the delivery of the plan and is developing specific, measurable actions under each of the points and will report on progress to the LSCB and its independent chair.

In addition, to secure a strategic regional approach, the police, local directors of children's services and the LSCB chairs have a programme of regular meetings to consider opportunities to cooperate across local authority borders to tackle CSE in the sub-region. The police and crime commissioner (PCC) is also represented at these meetings and is exploring ways to increase joint capacity to safeguard children from CSE and to prosecute perpetrators. As a result of this a number of initiatives, funded by the PCC, are being developed. These include the recruitment of a CSE safeguarding adviser and the recruitment for each local authority area of an officer to act as a single point of contact to ensure the effective sharing of information about CSE, missing children, persons of concern and trafficking intelligence across the region and to neighbouring sub-regions.

A national working group (NWG) on CSE has been established, to which the LSCB is affiliated. This provides a network for LSCB and partner organizations to share learning and experiences. Specific strands of work are led by the NWG to improve national arrangements for sharing information about emerging risks, missing children and trafficking issues. It is important that all organizations working to keep children safe from CSE are self-critical and seek opportunities to learn and improve services. The LSCB has a system of case audit and 'challenge panels' which allows for detailed analysis of the work done on cases and directly engages staff working on cases to learn from their experiences. These processes are in addition to quality assurance work undertaken by individual agencies. The LSCB has also been assisted by partners in getting the views of young people who have been identified as being at risk or abused through CSE. Some developments underway as a result of this activity include:

- the development of flow charts for professionals setting out CSE referral routes;

- a review of the current CSE referral and risk assessment tool;
- the revision of the LSCB strategic response to CSE to take account of feedback from professionals and young people, in particular young men and boys.

When appropriate, the LSCB and its partners undertake detailed learning reviews of cases for the purposes of improving services. One such review completed during 2014 concerned a case of a young person who was a victim of CSE and a prosecution witness in the trial of the perpetrator. As a result of the evidence given by this young woman the perpetrator was convicted. However, lessons were identified for police, children's services departments and the courts service. The young woman was a vulnerable witness facing significant obstacles in giving evidence. Due to her reluctance to give evidence she absconded from the court, a witness summons and a warrant for her arrest were issued, and she was held in police custody overnight before returning to court and giving evidence.

While there was much good practice identified in the review of the case, it was clear that single and joint agency working needed to be improved. Actions are underway to ensure that the police provide a specific officer, separate from the investigating officer, to give support to a vulnerable CSE witness in court proceedings. The joint planning arrangements for supporting young vulnerable witnesses have been strengthened to ensure that these are addressed explicitly and are not subsumed within other child in need, child protection or looked-after child planning processes. Children's services are working with other regional local authorities to identify potential arrangements for enhanced supervised accommodation for young people who are vulnerable witnesses if there is a risk that they may abscond or fail to attend court.

Discussions took place with the PCC regarding the wider availability of video links to courts to enable vulnerable witnesses to give evidence without the need to attend the court building. The independent chair of the LSCB and a senior officer from the police met the local judiciary to discuss learning from this case and an immediate action has been to change arrangements for the listing of such cases to minimize the risk of anxiety-provoking delays in witnesses being called to give evidence.

Responding to concerns about children and young people

A key part of the multi-agency response to CSE is that when there is a concern that a child or young person is at risk, a professional is required to complete a multi-agency CSE referral and risk assessment form and forward this to the multi-agency CSE Hub. Each morning, representatives of all of the services co-located in or working closely with the Hub meet to discuss all new referrals and to share information and update risk assessments of cases already known to the Hub. A shared assessment of risk is made on each case, which can be rated as low (preventative services to be provided by a single agency), medium (individual and family work to be offered which is likely to involve more than one agency) or high (a child has been abused or is at significant risk of being abused through CSE and requires a multi-agency plan and an active criminal investigation is required). As cases are reviewed the assessment of risk may go up or down. This is a key element of the multi-professional response.

At present, the council has a team manager and a social worker located in the Hub. The role of these staff is to ensure that appropriate risk assessments are completed and multi-agency child protection procedures are carried out on children that are referred to the Hub. These staff also ensure appropriate information-sharing and joint planning takes place between the Hub and the local authority social workers that are allocated to children at risk of CSE. This often involves supporting joint work with children and undertaking, with police colleagues, evidential interviews of child witnesses.

A police detective inspector, six detectives and two police constables are located in the Hub. These colleagues are responsible for criminal investigations of alleged CSE and working to build cases for prosecution. The police constables are also responsible for making enquiries about children who go missing from home or care and for gathering and monitoring information about missing episodes.

A voluntary sector project is located at the Hub which works with girls and boys to provide preventative inputs and to work directly with children, alongside partner services. A protocol with the district NHS care trust ensures that an identified, consistent sexual health nurse works with the Hub to support children, either at the Hub, in NHS premises or in the community. The activity of the Hub is supported by a police analyst and an administrative support worker.

In common with other children and adults who have been abused or are victims of violent crime, those who have experienced CSE are likely to require ongoing therapeutic support to assist them in recovery. The LSCB is working with partners in health trusts and the clinical commissioning groups (CCGs) to map current provision against a likely increase in demand. The outcome of this process may be that it is necessary to adjust current commissioning arrangements to ensure that CSE survivors have consistent access to relevant high quality services. Each district's Health and Well-being Board has a role in seeking assurance regarding arrangements for therapeutic support for CSE survivors.

Management information

As we saw in Chapter 10 the gathering and sharing of information is essential to effective multi-professional working. In the area being considered children's services staff can 'flag' cases of children at risk of CSE, to record information about individuals, location and premises that may present a risk of CSE in a way that complies with data protection requirements and facilitates the production of regular detailed reports about this activity. Prior to April 2014 it was not possible to produce detailed data reports other than by time-consuming manual processes. The police have developed a similar 'flagging' system which identifies for all officers and relevant police staff cases where there is a risk of CSE. The NHS 'System One' online records system is being gradually rolled out nationally: this already provides for enhanced information-sharing about child safeguarding matters within and between NHS trusts. At present, however, this system does not have the facility to 'flag' CSE concerns as distinct from other safeguarding concerns.

CSE is notoriously a hidden and under-reported social problem. In order that the reader can gauge the possible scale of the problem figures are provided here for the district considered in this chapter. Between 1 April and 30 September 2014, 158 children were referred to the Hub as being at risk of CSE. Of these children, 17 were under the age of 12, 30 were aged 12–13, 65 were 14–15 and 46 were over 16; 128 of the children were female and 30 were male. The ethnic breakdown of the group is: 99 white British, 19 other white backgrounds, 23 Asian and 14 mixed heritage. In three instances the ethnicity of the child was not recorded.

On 2 December 2014, 55 children were assessed by the Hub as being at high risk of CSE. Forty-nine of these children are female. Five or fewer of the children in this group are under 12, 27 are 13–15 years of age and 25 are over 16. Thirty of these children are of white British ethnicity, seven of other white ethnicity, eight identified as of Gypsy or Roma ethnicity, five or fewer of Asian ethnicity and five or fewer of mixed heritage.

Prosecution and disruption of CSE

The majority of CSE criminal investigations for the district are managed within the Hub. However, particularly complex and resource intensive investigations may be managed within the major enquiries team. At the time of writing one investigation from the district is being managed in this way as there are a significant number of potential perpetrators linked to this investigation.

The HUB CSE team undertake investigations that include situations where there is evidence of CSE and grooming taking place using the internet and social media, as well as 'street grooming'. At the time of writing (autumn 2015) there are 31 suspects, some of whom are currently on police bail, linked to these investigations. The ethnic origins of these suspects include Asian, white British and central or eastern European.

An important tool to disrupt the activity of suspected perpetrators of CSE is the Child Abduction Warning Notice. This was formerly known as a Harbourers' Warning. It can be issued against individuals who are suspected of grooming children by stating that they have no permission to associate with the named child and that if they do so they can be arrested under the Child Abduction Act 1984 and the Children Act 1989. Such warnings can be issued as a result of reasonable grounds for concern regarding a looked-after child up to the age of 18 and for other children up to the age of 16. In the district, 24 of these notices were issued during 2013–14.

Investigations into non-recent cases

As a result of increasing public awareness of CSE, particularly following the publication of the Jay Report, there has been a national increase in members of the public contacting local authorities and the police raising concerns about their own previous experiences of CSE, or about possible incidents of CSE that they may have witnessed in the past. Some members of the public have made contact with the council or police regarding past CSE incidents in the area.

A partnership approach has been developed to the issue of non-recent CSE concerns. A specialist team has been established: this consists of a detective sergeant, six constables, a police analyst, a police researcher, two social workers and a council researcher. Staffing levels for this service are being kept under review. The service has clear terms of reference which have been agreed by partner organizations.

Community safety implications

CSE can be seen as a violent criminal activity. The consequences of CSE can be long-standing for the victim and there is growing research evidence that victims of CSE are themselves over-represented among young people coming to the attention of police services as potential offenders. In addition, CSE has lasting consequences for families of victims and perpetrators and has potential implications for community relations. The Community Safety Partnership received a presentation about CSE delivered by the LSCB CSE Champion and the assistant director for specialist children's services. The approach taken to community safety included:

- a request that each area committee receives a report regarding CSE;
- approval of the establishment of the historic CSE team;
- approval of the LSCB nine-point strategic response to CSE outlined earlier in this chapter;
- endorsement of work to widen school initiatives to develop an appropriate package for use in primary schools;
- approval of the programme of CSE training for council staff in licensing, hackney cab, environmental health, city solicitors and housing, and other relevant regulatory services within the locality;
- approval of a similar, targeted CSE awareness-raising and training programme for the council's front-line uniformed staff who work on the local streets.

Conclusion

This chapter has explored in detail how one local authority area has developed a partnership approach based in multi-professional work. It has demonstrated that multi-professional work is essential in developing a comprehensive approach to CSE. The challenges are many – from prevention to prosecution – all of which require multi-professional work.

Think point

This chapter has argued and demonstrated that multi-professional working is essential in tackling child sexual exploitation. Suggest three arguments that support this point.

13

Taking multi-professional practice forward

Nick Frost and Mark Robinson

Introduction

This book has outlined and analysed findings from the MATCh research project on multi-professional teams working with children and their families and then moved on to explore a range of related contemporary challenges in the field of child welfare and multi-professional working. We have drawn on the empirical findings from a research project, contemporary research and practice findings, and theoretical frameworks that helped design the study and make sense of our findings. We have also attempted to address the reality of contemporary policy and practice development in multi-professional working through a number of focused chapters. We hope that as a whole this book provides a study of the state of the art in relation to multi-professional teamwork with children and young people.

The aim of this final chapter is to be more speculative and to offer a contribution to the current policy debates about work with children and young people in multi-disciplinary settings.

It is argued here that the turning point in British child welfare was provided by the New Labour Every Child Matters agenda. Every Child Matters embodied the most profound policy shifts in child welfare and health policy since 1989, when children's services were fundamentally reformed. Tony Blair in his prime ministerial foreword to *Every Child Matters* (DfES 2003:2) wrote:

> Responding to the inquiry headed by Lord Laming into Victoria's death, we are proposing here a range of measures to reform and improve children's care – crucially, for the first time ever requiring local authorities to bring together in one place under one person services for children, and at the same

time suggesting real changes in the way those we ask to do this work carry
out their tasks on our and our children's behalf.

This provided a holistic approach to modern childhood which underlined the
importance of a comprehensive, integrated and multi-professional approach to
service provision. Every Child Matters led to new organizational structures and,
as we argue throughout this book, a profound and lasting shift in the professional
mind-set. We hope this third edition of this book has demonstrated the long-term
impact of these changes.

Exploring relationships between the processes of public services and their
products or outcomes has always bedevilled both government monitoring of the
effects of changes in social policy and research into effectiveness. In 2003, a systematic review of research evidence of joint working (Cameron and Lart 2003)
found 32 studies that fitted with inclusion criteria. Cameron and Lart's discussion
of evidence of joint working was presented under three themes: organizational,
cultural, and professional and contextual issues. Their tentative conclusion was
that there was some association between the type of model of joint working and the
factors promoting and obstacles hindering progress. However, they admitted
that within the studies there was limited evidence on effectiveness, and that our
knowledge as to what constitutes effective joint working between health and
social services has hardly moved on since studies in the late 1970s and early 1980s.

A similar scepticism is demonstrated by Glisson and Hemmelgarn (1998)
who undertook a rigorous, quasi-experimental study of the impact of integrated
approaches on outcomes for children. These authors struggled to find positive outcomes of integrated working and they conclude that: 'Efforts to improve public
children's service systems should focus on creating positive organizational climates
rather than on increasing interorganizational services coordination' (1998: 401).

Despite these and other forms of tenuous research evidence of 'what works',
the rollercoaster of reforms in public services developed apace under New
Labour. Since then researchers have become more positive about the impact of
multi-professional working. The Local Authority Research Consortium (LARC5)
(Easton et al. 2013) studies are optimistic in their findings about the process and
outcomes of multi-professional work in the context of early intervention and the
tool known as the Common Assessment Framework.

These key messages will permeate the discussion in this chapter. However,
we will structure our discussion of how multi-professional practice will be taken
forward around a diagrammatic representation of integrated services promoted
by the New Labour government (1997–2010): we argue that this remains perti-
nent and helpful today. The diagram (see Figure 13.1) is known colloquially as
'the onion'. It is significant that outcomes for children, young people and their
parents are metaphorically at the centre of the onion. Here we can see the commitment of the then government to developing and strengthening the Children's
Trust model – and therefore their belief that integrated working can actually

Figure 13.1 The 'onion' of integrated services

deliver improved outcomes for children and young people. The imperative for further integration and coordination was driven even more strongly after the tragic death of Baby Peter (Laming 2009).

Inter-agency governance

At the level of the English government we have witnessed a number of government reorganizations with responsibility for children's services having been reshaped into an infrastructure that leads and reflects an integrated services approach. Perhaps most significantly, in 2007, it was decided to follow the logic of the policy direction and form the Department for Children, Schools and Families, under the leadership of Ed Balls. This brought together the major issues facing children and young people in one powerful central government department. This direction was at least partially diverted by the decision in 2010 to rename this department as the Department for Education – symbolically undermining the commitment to multi-professional approaches.

The coalition government (2010–15), as we saw in Chapter 1, has partially dismantled these structures – while paradoxically multi-professional working is flourishing at the local level.

Integrated strategy

One of the survivors of the Every Child Matters strategy has been the multi-professional plan in each local authority area: while they have the core purpose of giving a clear strategy for each area, they have varying titles, structures and approaches. They also have to be read in tandem with a range of other strategies which may emerge from the Local Safeguarding Children Boards (LSCBs), Health and Well-being Boards and Community Safety Partnerships, for example. Integrated strategy, then, is alive and well at local authority level – if rather missing at central government level.

Integrated processes

A key concern for implementing integrated services is how outcomes will be monitored and measured and how information will be shared across agencies, as we have seen in Chapter 10 in particular. The key integrated processes under New Labour – the Common Assessment Framework and Contact Point – are now firmly in the past, but most local authority areas have integrated processes firmly embedded in local areas, around their early intervention offer, MASH and hubs.

Integrated front-line delivery

It is integrated front-line delivery that has flourished most in recent years – in this book we have explored hubs, MASH and youth offending teams, for example. As we have seen in our MATCh findings, professionals seem to enjoy such co-located working and believe it can contribute to better outcomes for children, young people and their families.

Outcomes for children and young people, their families and communities

What really matters in the reform of public services and the rollout of multi-professional practice is that the delivery of services for children and their families is better than it was, and results in enhanced outcomes for them. Throughout this book evidence has been provided that outcomes are rising from the process of multi-professional working. The hope is that books like this will continue the debate about what we can do to address poor outcomes and life chances for children, and how as professionals, researchers and policy-makers with responsibility for delivering services we can play our part in improving them.

Leadership

Leadership is essential in taking initiatives for integrated children's services – as we saw in Chapter 9 of this book, in particular. Considerable energy has been put into developing the leadership of children's services through the National Centre for Schools Leadership, the Association of Directors of Children's Services

(ADCS) , SOLACE (the Society of Local Authority Chief Executives), central and local government and in academia. In England there is now a cadre of children's services leaders that did not exist at the end of the twentieth century. This group face many challenges of leading multi-disciplinary services, in a high profile role, in a rapidly changing and challenging service provision environment. The turnover of people since the DCS role was introduced in 2004 has been remarkably high, with them often moving on following a critical inspection or media scrutiny following serious incidents. Developing the next generation of 'joined-up' leaders will be central if the ideas in this book are to be taken forward.

Addressing 'wicked' social problems

The major driver towards the increasing extent of integrated working is the persistence of 'wicked' social problems (Stewart 1997). These are social problems with no obvious solutions and where actions may lead to unintended consequences. These problems may be long-standing (e.g. crime), outside the immediate control of social agencies (e.g. obesity) or very complex to tackle (e.g. child sexual exploitation). They are not amenable to an easy or straightforward solution or approach. Wicked problems in relation to children and young people usually involve the concerns of a wide range of professionals – police, social care, health, education and the voluntary sector, for example.

Integrated working: a way forward?

Where next for integrated working? The forces outlined above are powerful and we believe that integrated working will continue to grow and develop. We suggest the following as key elements if we are to work towards a positive future for multi-professional teamwork:

- Continuing to develop a strong, cross-sector leadership group. The ADCS, the National College for Teaching and Leadership, the Virtual College and others have made a valuable contribution towards building such strong leadership cadre. Such leaders need to work across traditional professional and organizational boundaries, requiring a particular set of leadership skills which in turn require nurturing and support.

- Building on the achievements of the existing structures – such as Children's Trusts and LSCBs. These structures bring a diverse group of sector-based leaders together under the guidance of a 'boundary spanning' leader – an independent chair of an LSCB, for example.

- One of the notable developments of the post-2004 period has been the, largely uncharted, growth of multi-disciplinary, co-located teams, often referred to as MASHs or hubs. These vary according to funding, leadership, focus and (co-)location, include two or more different professional groups, and focus on a particular issue, such as assessment or child sexual exploitation (see Chapter 12 for example). These teams provide an excellent base for effective multi-professional teamwork.

- The continuing development of a research and evaluation base. As we have seen in this book, during the 1990s and early 2000s researchers were often sceptical about the benefits of multi-professional working to service users. More optimistic findings merged from 2006 onwards – including the first edition of this book which was positive about the impact on professionals up to and including the LARC 1–5 studies.

- Progressing workforce development in multi-professional methods will be essential. Currently the picture is patchy: for example, most pre-qualifying training in universities is 'silo-based' – teachers, social workers and health visitors, for example, may be in the same university but train separately. Many universities bring such students together under the banner of programmes often called 'inter-professional learning' (IPL), but these programmes add up to days rather than weeks. Continuing professional development (CPD) is perhaps more embedded in multi-professional approaches. There are two primary methods for CPD being delivered to child welfare professionals. One is silo-based – CPD undertaken to meet the need of the professional associations and to address the criteria for professional registration. The other major route is multi-disciplinary as it is delivered by LSCBs. Most LSCBs employ training officers who deliver multi-agency training to a wide range of professionals, who are represented at the LSCB. The advantage of this training is that it usually brings together a wide range of professionals working with children and young people. A potential disadvantage is that this training tends to be focused on 'child protection' issues rather than 'child welfare' as a wider and more inclusive social practice.

- Underpinning these are the more complex issues around values. A commitment to multi-professional working and to striving towards the best interests of children and young people is based in the values of professionals. The best multi-professional workers have a profound value orientation towards working together in the best interests of children and young people.

We hope that this book has provided a small contribution to sustaining multi-professional working.

Appendix: Multi-agency team checklist

David Cottrell, Angela Anning, Nick Frost,
Jo Green and Mark Robinson

This checklist is derived from the results of the MATCh project exploring the functioning of multi-agency teams. Team members should complete the checklist individually and teams should then discuss the findings collectively. Results may indicate areas of team function that need to be clarified with stakeholder agencies and/or areas of team function that would benefit from more discussion within the team. Where there is divergence of views within a team, members should consider why this is and whether changes to the way the team operates would facilitate team functioning.

Domain 1: structural – systems and management	Strongly disagree/ never	Disagree/ sometimes	Agree/ often	Strongly agree/ always
The team has clear objectives that have been agreed by all stakeholding agencies				
The team has clear workload targets that have been agreed by all stakeholding agencies				
The team has the authority to make decisions about day-to-day team function (as long as in accord with agreed targets and objectives)				
There is clarity about line management arrangements for all team members				
There are clear mechanisms for coordinating the work of team members				

cont.

Domain 1: structural – systems and management (continued)	Strongly disagree/ never	Disagree/ sometimes	Agree/ often	Strongly agree/ always
Clear mechanisms exist to inform part-time team members about what has taken place in their absence				
Team members are co-located in shared buildings				
Structures exist for communication with all stakeholding agencies (e.g. a steering group)				
Stakeholding agencies have made transparent efforts to minimize inequalities caused by different terms and conditions of service for team members employed by different agencies				
Domain 2: ideological – sharing and redistributing knowledge/skills/beliefs				
Different theoretical models are respected within the team				
Different professional groups are accorded equal respect within the team				
Supervision of work is attuned to the needs of the individuals within the team and their various professional backgrounds				
The team encourages members to share skills and ideas with each other				
The team has an awareness of the potential impact of multi-agency working on both professional identity and service users				

cont.

Domain 3: participation in developing new processes	Strongly disagree/ never	Disagree/ sometimes	Agree/ often	Strongly agree/ always
The team has been able to develop new processes and procedures in order to meet its agreed objectives				
Team members do not necessarily have to follow inappropriate agency of origin procedures where they conflict with agreed team objectives				
Opportunities exist for team members to have time away from the immediacy of delivering services in order to reflect on practice and develop new ways of working (e.g. team away days, joint team training events)				
The team engages in joint client-focused activities such as shared assessment and/or consultation with families				
There are regular opportunities for whole team discussion of client-focused activities				
Stakeholding agencies continue to provide ongoing support for the professional development of their staff in multi-agency teams as well as supporting team development activities				
Domain 4: inter-professional – learning through role change				
The team has good and clear leadership				
Roles within the team are clear				

cont.

Domain 4: inter-professional – learning through role change (continued)	Strongly disagree/ never	Disagree/ sometimes	Agree/ often	Strongly agree/ always
The team does not allow certain individuals or professional groups to dominate the team				
The contribution of part-time team members is acknowledged				
The team allows individual members to retain and develop their 'specialist' skills				
Team members are able to learn new ways of practising from each other				

There are no right answers but teams where most members tend to agree with the statements above are likely to function more efficiently and effectively.

Bibliography

Allen, G. (2011) *Early Intervention: Smart Investment, Massive Savings. The second report to HM Government*. London: The Cabinet Office.

Ancona, D., Malone, T.W., Orlikowski, W.J. and Senge, P.M. (2007) In praise of the incomplete leader, *Harvard Business Review*, February: 94–9.

Anning, A. and Ball, M. (2008) *Improving Children's Services*. London: Sage Publications Ltd.

Argyris, C. and Schön, D.A. (1976) *Theory in Practice*. San Francisco: Jossey-Bass.

Atkinson, M., Jones, M. and Lamont, E. (2007) *Multi-agency Working and its Implications for Practice: A Review of the Literature*. London: CfBT, Education Trust.

Atkinson, M., Wilkin, A., Scott, A. and Kinder, K. (2001) *Multi-Agency Activity: An Audit of Activity, Local Government Association Research, Report 17*. Slough: National Foundation for Education and Research.

ATL (Association of Teachers and Lecturers) (2003) *Raising Standards and Tackling the Workload*. London: DfES.

Audit Commission (1996) *Misspent Youth*. London: Audit Commission.

Audit Commission (2004) *Youth Justice 2004: A Review of the Reformed Youth Justice System*. London: Audit Commission.

Baines, S., Wilson, R. and Walsh, S. (2010) Seeing the full picture? Technologically enabled multi-agency working in health and social care, *New Technology, Work and Employment*, 25(1): 19–33.

Balls, E. (2007) Disabled children must stay top of the agenda, *Community Care*, 6 December: 23.

Barton, A. and Quinn, C. (2002) Risk management of groups or respect for the individual? Issues for information sharing and confidentiality in drug treatment and testing orders, *Drugs: Education Prevention and Policy*, 9(1): 35–43.

Bax, M. and Whitmore, K. (1991) District handicap teams in England: 1983–8, *Archives of Disease in Childhood*, 66: 656–64.

BBC News (2014) Rotherham abuse scandal: children's services director Joyce Thacker quits, 19 September. Accessed 21 September 2014 at: http://www.bbc.co.uk/news/uk-england-29286638

Belsky, J., Barnes, J. and Melhuish, E. (eds) (2007) *The National Evaluation of Sure Start: Does Area-based Early Intervention Work?* Bristol: The Policy Press.

Bercow, J. (2008) *The Bercow Report: a review of services for children and young people (0–19) with speech, language and communication needs*. London: DCSF.

Bilson, A. (ed.) (2005) *Evidence-based Practice in Social Work*. London: Whiting & Birch.

Bradbury, H., Frost, N., Kilminster, S. and Zukas, M. (2010) *Beyond Reflective Practice*. London: Routledge.

Brandon, M. et al. (2008) *Analysing Child Deaths and Serious Injury through Abuse and Neglect: What Can We Learn? A Biennial Analysis of Serious Case Reviews 2003–05*. London: Department of Children, Schools and Families, DCSF-RR023.

Bronfenbrenner, U. (1979) *The Ecology of Human Development: Experiments by Nature and Design*. Cambridge, MA: Harvard University Press.

BSRM/RCP (2003) *Rehabilitation Following Brain Injury: National Clinical Guidelines*. London: Royal College of Physicians.

Burt, R.S. (1992) *Structural Holes: The Social Structure of Competition*. Cambridge, MA: Harvard University Press.

Cabinet Office (2006) *Reaching Out: An Action Plan on Social Exclusion*. London: Cabinet Office Social Exclusion Task Force.

Cameron, A. and Lart, R. (2003) Factors promoting and obstacles hindering joint working: a systematic review of the research evidence, *Journal of Integrated Care*, 11(2).

Castells, M. (1998) *The End of the Millennium*. Oxford: Blackwell.

CEIS (Centre of Excellence for Information Sharing) (2014) Accessed 30 September 2014 at: www.informationsharing.co.uk

Chesterman, D. and Horne, M. (2002) Local authority? How to develop leadership for better public services. London: DEMOS.

Children and Society (2009) Special issue: the outcomes of integrated working for children and young people.

Cornish, J. (2015) *Improving Transition for Children and Young People*. London: NHS England.

Cottrell, D. and Kramm, A. (2005) Growing Up? A History of CAMHS (1987–2005), *Child and Adolescent Mental Health*, 10(3): 111–17.

Council for Disabled Children (2011) *Every Disabled Child Matters: Response to the Government Equalities Office Consultation Equality Act 2010: The Public Sector Equality Duty: Reducing Bureaucracy, Policy Review Paper*. London: Government Equalities Office.

CQC (Care Quality Commission) (2014) *From the Pond into the Sea: children's transitions to adult health services*. Newcastle: CQC.

Craston, M., Thom, G., Spivack, R., Lambert, C., Yorath, F., Purdon, S., Bryson, C., Sheikh, S. and Smith, L. (2013a) *Impact Evaluation of the SEND Pathfinder Programme. Research Report*. London: TSO.

Craston, M., Thom, G. and Spivack, R. (2013b) *Evaluation of the SEND Pathfinder Programme: process and implementation research brief*. London: TSO.

Craston, M., Macmillan, T., Hill, K. and Carr, C. (2014) *Evaluation of the SEND Pathfinder Programme Thematic Report: Collaborative working with health*. London: SQW.

Cross, M. (2006) A spineless performance, *Guardian*, Thursday 12 January.

Dartington Social Research Unit (2004) *Refocusing Children's Services Toward Prevention: Lessons from the Literature* (DfES Research Report 510). London: DfES. Accessed 6 December 2007 at: http://www.dfes.gov.uk/research/data/upload files/RR510.pdf.

Dawes, S., Cresswell, A. and Pardo T. (2009) From 'need to know' to 'need to share'. Tangled problems, information boundaries, and the building of public sector knowledge networks, *Public Administration Review*, 69(3): 392–402.

DCA (Department for Constitutional Affairs) (2003) *Public Sector Data Sharing: Guidance on the Law*. London: Department for Constitutional Affairs.

DCLG (Department for Communities and Local Government) (2012) *Working with Troubled Families: A Guide to the Evidence and Good Practice*. Accessed 10 July 2014 at: https://www.gov.uk/government/uploads/system/uploads/attachment_data/file/66113/121214_Working_with_troubled_families_FINAL_v2.pdf

DCSF (Department for Children, Schools and Families) (2007a) *The Children's Plan*. London: DCSF.

DCSF (Department for Children, Schools and Families) (2007b) *Aiming Higher for Disabled Children*. London: DCSF.

DCSF (Department for Children, Schools and Families) (2007c) *Care Matters: A Time for Change*. London: DCSF.

DCSF (Department for Children, Schools and Families) (2008a) *Aiming High for Young People*. London: DCSF.

DCSF (Department for Children, Schools and Families) (2008b) *Children's Trusts: Statutory Guidance*. London: DCSF.

DCSF (Department for Children, Schools and Families) (2008c) *The 21st Century School: A Transformation in Education*. London: DCSF.

DCSF (Department for Children, Schools and Families) (2008d) *Care Matters: Time to Deliver for Children in Care*. London: DCSF.

DCSF (Department for Children, Schools and Families) (2008e) *Building Brighter Futures: Next Steps for the Children's Workforce*. London: DCSF.

DCSF (Department for Children, Schools and Families) (2009) *Statutory Guidance. The Roles and Responsibilities of the Lead Member for Children's Services and the Director of Children's Services*. Nottingham: DCSF Publications.

DCSF (Department for Children, Schools and Families) (2010) *Working Together to Safeguard Children*. London: DCSF.

DCSF/DoH (Department for Children, Schools and Families/Department of Health) (2008) *Children and Young People in Mind: The Final Report of the National CAMHS Review*. London: DCSF.

Dent, M. and Tutt, D. (2014) Electronic patient information systems and care pathways: the organisational challenges of implementation and integration, *Health Informatics Journal*, 20(3): 176–88.

Department for Children, Schools and Families (DCSF)/Home Office (2009) *Safeguarding Children and Young People from Sexual Exploitation: Supplementary Guidance to Working Together to Safeguard Children*. London: DCSF.

Department for Communities and Local Government (2015) Report of Inspection of Rotherham Metropolitan Borough Council (author Louise Casey CB). Accessed 12 December 2015 at: www.gov.uk/government/publications

DES (Department of Education and Science) (1978) *The Report of the Committee of Enquiry into the Education of Handicapped Children and Young People* (the Warnock Report). London: HMSO.

DETR (Department of the Environment, Transport and Regions) (1999) *Modernising Local Government: Guidance for the Local Government Act 1999, Best Value*. London: DETR.

DfE (Department for Education) (2011a) *Tackling Child Sexual Exploitation: Action Plan*. London: The Stationary Office.

DfE (Department for Education) (2011b) *A Child-Centred System: the Government's response to the Munro Review of child protection*. London: TSO.

DfE (Department for Education) (2011c) *Support and Aspiration: a new approach to special educational needs and disability. A consultation*. London: TSO.

DfE (Department for Education) (2012) *Support and Aspiration: A New Approach to Special Educational Needs and Disability – Progress and Next Steps*. London: TSO.

DfE (Department for Education) (2013) *Working Together to Safeguard Children: A Guide to Inter-agency Working to Safeguard and Promote the Welfare of Children*. London: The Stationery Office.

DfE (Department for Education) (2015) *Working Together to Safeguard Children: A Guide to Inter-agency Working to Safeguard and Promote the Welfare of Children*. London: The Stationery Office.

DfE/DoH (Department for Education/Department of Health) (2015) *Special Educational Needs and Disability Code of Practice: 0–25 years. Statutory guidance for organisations which work with and support children and young people who have special educational needs or disabilities*. London: TSO.

DfES (Department for Education and Skills) (2001) *Special Educational Needs Code of Practice*. Nottingham: DfES.

DfES (Department for Education and Skills) (2003) *Every Child Matters*. London: HMSO.

DfES (Department for Education and Skills) (2004) *Every Child Matters: Change for Children*. London: HMSO.

DfES (Department for Education and Skills) (2005) *Youth Matters*. London: HMSO.

DfES (Department for Education and Skills) (2006) *Care Matters: Transforming the Lives of Children and Young People in Care*. London: HMSO.

DfES/DoH (Department for Education and Skills/Department of Health) (2002a) *Together from the Start: Practical Guidance for Professionals Working with Disabled Children (0–2) and their Families*. London: HMSO.

DfES/DoH (Department for Education and Skills/Department of Health) (2002b) *Developing Early Intervention/Support Services for Deaf Children and their Families*. London: HMSO.

DfES/DoH (Department for Education and Skills/Department of Health) (2004a) *The National Framework for Children, Young People and Maternity Services*. London: DoH.

DfES/DoH (Department for Education and Skills/Department of Health) (2004b) *Acquired Brain Injury*. London: Department of Health.

DfES/DoH (Department for Education and Skills/Department of Health) (2007) *Children's Trust Pathfinders: innovative partnerships for improving the well-being of children and young people. National Evaluation of Children's Trust Pathfinders, Final Report*. Norwich: University of East Anglia in association with the National Children's Bureau.

DoH (Department of Health) (1976) *Fit for the Future: Report of the Committee on Child Health Services* (The Court Report, Cmnd 6684, vol. 1). London: HMSO.

DoH (Department of Health) (2000) *Safeguarding Children Involved in Prostitution*. London: DoH.

DoH (Department of Health) (2001a) *Hospital Episode Statistics, 2000/2001*. London: DoH.

DoH (Department of Health) (2001b) *Valuing People: A New Strategy for Learning Disabilities for the 21st century – a White Paper*. London: TSO.

DoH (Department of Health) (2005) *Commissioning a Patient-led NHS*. London: DoH.

DoH (Department of Health) (2008a) *Child Health Strategy*. London: DoH.

DoH (Department of Health) (2008b) *High Quality Care for All: NHS Next Stage Review*, the Darzi Report. London: DoH.

DoH (Department of Health) (2010) *The Kennedy Review: Getting It Right for Children and Young People – overcoming cultural barriers in the NHS so as to meet their needs*. London: TSO.

DoH (Department of Health) (2012) *The Mandate: A Mandate from the Government to the NHS Commissioning Board – April 2013 to March 2015*. London: TSO.

DoH (Department of Health) (2013) *Improving Children and Young People's Health Outcomes: a system wide response*. London: TSO.

DoH/DCSF (Department of Health/Department for Children, Schools and Families) (2008) *The Child Health Promotion Programme*. London: DoH.

DoH (Department of Health), National Assembly for Wales, Home Office, Department for Education and Employment (2000) *Safeguarding Children Involved in Prostitution: Supplementary Guidance to Working Together to Safeguard Children*. London: DoH.

Dunleavy, P. (2010) *The Future of Joined-up Public Services*. London: 2020 Public Services Trust.

Durham County Council (and County Durham Children and Family Partnership) (2014) *County Durham Practice Framework: single assessment procedure and practice guidance*. Durham: Durham County Council.

Eason, K. and Waterson, P. (2013) Fitness for purpose when there are many different purposes: who are electronic patient records for? *Health Informatics Journal*, 82[s] e9b-e10b.

Easton, C., Lamont, L., Smith, R. and Aston, H. (2013). '*We Should Have Been Helped from Day One': a Unique Perspective from Children, Families and Practitioners*. Findings from LARC5. Slough: NFER.

Edwards, A. and Fox, C. (2005) Using activity theory to evaluate a complex response to social exclusion, *Educational and Child Psychology*, 22(1): 50–61.

Engestrom, Y. (ed.) (1999) *Perspectives on Activity Theory*. New York: Cambridge University Press.

Engestrom, Y. (2000) Making expansive decisions: an activity theoretical study of practitioners building collaborative medical care for children, in K. Allwood and M. Selart (eds) *Creative Decision Making in the Social World*. Amsterdam: Kluwer.

Engestrom, Y. (2001) Expansive learning at work: toward an activity theoretical reconceptualization, *Journal of Education and Work*, 14(1): 133–56.

Engestrom, Y., Engestrom, R. and Vahaaho, T. (1999) When the center does not hold: the importance of knotworking, in S. Chaiklin, M. Hedegaard and U. Jensen (eds) *Activity Theory and Social Practice*. Aarhus: Aarhus University Press.

Eraut, M. (1999) Non-formal learning in the workplace: the hidden dimension of lifelong learning. A framework for analysis and the problems it poses for researchers. Paper presented at the First International Conference on Researching Work and Learning, University of Leeds.

Farmakopoulou, N. (2002) 'What lies underneath?' An inter-organisational analysis of collaboration between education and social work, *British Journal of Social Work*, 32(8).

Frost, N. (2001) Professionalism, change and the politics of lifelong learning, *Studies in Continuing Education*, 23(1): 5–17.

Frost, N. (2005) *Professionalism, Partnership and Joined Up Thinking*. Dartington: Research in Practice.

Frost, N. (2009) Leading children's services: some contemporary issues and challenges, *The Journal of Children's Services*, 4(3), November: 49–57.

Frost, N. (2011) *Rethinking Children and Families*. London: Continuum.

Frost, N. (2014a) Interagency working with children and families: what works and what makes a difference?' in P. Foley and A. Rixon (eds) *Changing Children's Services: Working and Learning Together*, 2nd edn. Bristol: Policy Press.

Frost, N. (2014b) Children's services: the changing workplace?' in P. Foley and A. Rixon (eds) *Changing Children's Services: Working and Learning Together*, 2nd edn. Bristol: Policy Press.

Frost, N. and Lloyd, A. (2006) Implementing multi-disciplinary teamwork in the new child welfare policy environment, *Journal of Integrated Care*, 14: 2.

Frost, N. and Parton, N. (2009) *Understanding Children's Social Care*. London: Sage.

Frost, N., Robinson, M. and Anning, A. (2005) Social workers in multi-disciplinary teams: issues and dilemmas for professional practice, *Child & Family Social Work*, 10(3), August: 187–96.

Garrett, L. and Lodge, S. (2009) *Integrated Practice on the Front Line*. Dartington: Research in Practice.

Garrett, P.M. (2005) Social work's 'electronic turn', *Critical Social Policy*, 25(4): 529–53.

George, N., Hetherington, M. and Sharp, C. (2011) *Local Authorities' Perceptions of How Parents and Young People with Special Educational Needs will be Affected by the 2011 Green Paper. Local Government Group Research Report*. Slough: NFER.

Glass, N. (1999) Sure Start: the development of an early intervention programme for young children in the UK, *Children & Society*, 13: 257–64.

Glisson, C. and Hemmelgarn, A. (1998) The effects of organizational climate and interorganizational coordination on the quality and outcomes of children's service systems, *Child Abuse and Neglect*, 22(5): 401–21.

Government Chief Social Researcher's Office (2005) *Trying It Out: The Role of 'Pilots' in Policy-Making*. London: Cabinet Office.

Granville, J. and Langton, P. (2002) Working across boundaries: systemic and psychodynamic perspectives on multi-disciplinary and inter-agency practice, *Journal of Social Work Practice*, 16(1): 23–7.

Greenberg, D. and Shroder, M. (1997) *The Digest of Social Experiments*, 2nd edn. Washington, DC: Urban Institute Press.

Guardian (2009) Full statement by leader of Haringey council, 1 May. Accessed 24 January 2010 at: http://www.guardian.co.uk/society/2009/may/01/baby-p-haringey-council-statement

Guardian (2011) The Right Line for Social Care. The *Guardian* Roundtable in association with the Voluntary Organisations' Disability Group, 27 July.

Hall, D. (1997) Child development teams: are they fulfilling their purpose? *Child: Care, Health and Development*, 23: 87–99.

Harré, R. (1983) *Personal Being*. Oxford: Blackwell.

Haywood, J. (2005) Vision and the challenges ahead, *Partners*, 41: 2–3.

Hill, K., Thom, G., Carr, C. and Agbr. M. (2014) *Evaluation of the SEND Pathfinder Programme Thematic Report: Engagement of schools Research report*. London: SQW.

Home Office (1998) *Interdepartmental Circular on Establishing Youth Offending Teams*, 22 December. London: Home Office.

Home Office (2000) *Report of Policy Action Team 12: Young People*. London: HMSO.

House of Commons Education and Skills Committee (2006) *Special Educational Needs – Third Report of Session 2005–06, Vol. 1*. London: TSO.

Hudson, B. (2002) Interprofessionality in health and social care: the Achilles' heel of partnership, *Journal of Interprofessional Care*, 16(1).

Jamieson, A. and Owen, S. (2000) *Ambition for Change: Partnerships, Children and Work*. London: National Children's Bureau.

Jenkins, R. (2002) *Social Identity*. London: Routledge.

Jenks, C. (1996) *Childhood*. London: Routledge

Kay, A. and Teasdale, G. (2001) Head injury in the United Kingdom, *World Journal of Surgery*, 25: 1210–20.

Lamb, B. (2009) *Lamb Enquiry: Special Educational Needs and Parental Confidence*. London: DCSF.

Laming, H. (2003) *The Victoria Climbié Inquiry*. London: HMSO.

Laming, H. (2009) *The Protection of Children in England: A Progress Report*. London: The Stationery Office.

Lave, J. and Wenger, E. (1991) *Situated Learning: Legitimate Peripheral Participation*. Cambridge: Cambridge University Press.

Lord, P., Kinder, K., Wilkin, A., Atkinson, M. and Harland, J. (2008) *Evaluating the Early Impact of Integrated Children's Services*. Round 1 final report. Slough: NFER.

Lownsborough, H. and O'Leary, D. (2005) *The Leadership Imperative, Reforming Children's Services from the Ground Up*. London: DEMOS.

Loxley, A. (1997) *Collaboration in Health and Welfare: Working in Difference*. London: Jessica Kingsley.

Maltby, B. (2007) *How Does Leadership Make a Difference to Organisational Culture and Effectiveness? An Overview for the Public Sector*. Northern Leadership Academy. Accessed 12 December 2015 at: www.northernleadershipacademy.co.uk

Miller, C. and McNicholl, A. (2003) *Integrating Children's Services: Issues and Practice*. London: Office of Public Management.

Mott MacDonald (2015) Engagement and participation. SEND Pathfinder information pack v6, March 2015. Accessed 12 December 2015 at: http://www.sendpathfinder.co.uk/engagement-and-participation-information-pack

Munro, E. (2011a) *The Munro Review of Child Protection Part One: A Systems Analysis*. London: The Stationery Office.

Munro, E. (2011b) *The Munro Review of Child Protection Interim Report: The Child's Journey*. London: The Stationery Office.

Munro, E. (2011c) *The Munro Review of Child Protection: Final Report: A Child-centred System*. London: The Stationery Office.

Munro, E. and Lushey, C. (2012) *The impact of more flexible assessment practices in response to the Munro Review of Child Protection: Emerging findings from the trials*. London: Childhood Wellbeing Research Centre.

NECF (National Evaluation of Children's Fund) (2004) *Developing Collaboration in Preventative Services for Children and Young People: The First Annual Report of NECF*. London: DfES.

NECT (National Evaluation of Children's Trusts) (2005) *Realising Children's Trust Arrangements: The Full Phase 1 Report*. London: DfES.

NECTP (National Evaluation of Children's Trusts Pathfinders) (2007) *Children's Trusts Pathfinders: Innovative Partnerships for Improving the Wellbeing of Children*. London: DfES.

NESS (National Evaluation of Sure Start) (2004) *Implementing Sure Start Local Programmes: Full Report, Part 1 and Part 2*. London: HMSO.

NESS (National Evaluation of Sure Start) (2005a) *Early Impacts of Sure Start Local Programmes on Children and Families*, Report 013. London: HMSO.

NESS (National Evaluation of Sure Start) (2005b) *Implementing Sure Start Local Programmes: An Integrated Overview of the First Four Years*. London: HMSO.

NESS (National Evaluation of Sure Start) (2005c) *Variation in Sure Start Local Programme Effectiveness: Early Preliminary Findings*, Report 014. London: HMSO.

NESS (National Evaluation of Sure Start) (2005d) *Report on the Case Studies of the Implementation Module: National Evaluation of Sure Start*. London: HMSO.

NESS (National Evaluation of Sure Start) (2008) *The Impact of Sure Start Local Programmes on Three Year Olds and Their Families*. London: HMSO.

Newcastle City Council and Skills for People (2015) *The Big Handbook: a guide to individual budgets in Newcastle*. Newcastle: Newcastle City Council.

NHS/HAS (National Health Service/Health Advisory Service) (1995) *Child & Adolescent Mental Health Services: Together We Stand*. London: HAS.

NICE (National Institute for Health and Clinical Excellence) (2003) *Head Injury: Triage, Assessment, Investigation and Early Management of Head Injury in Infants, Children and Adolescents*. London: NICE.

Office of the Children's Commissioner for England (2012–13) *Inquiry into Child Sexual Exploitation by Gangs and Groups* (three reports and three additional documents). Accessed 6 June 2015 at: http://www.childrenscommissioner.gov.uk/info/csegg1

Ofsted (2009a) *Comprehensive Area Assessment: Annual Rating of Council Children's Services for 2009*. London: Ofsted.

Ofsted (2009b) *Unannounced Inspections of Contact, Referral and Assessment*. London: Ofsted.

Ofsted (2009c) *Inspections of Safeguarding and Looked-after Children Services*. London: Ofsted.

Ofsted (2014) *Thematic Inspection: The child sexual exploitation of children: it couldn't happen here, could it?* Accessed 6 June 2015 at: http://www.ofsted.gov.uk/resources/sexual-exploitation-of-children-it-couldnt-happen-here-could-it

Øvretveit, J. (1993) *Coordinating Community Care: Multidisciplinary Teams and Care Management*. Buckingham: Open University Press.

Parton, D. (2008) Integrated teams: how well do they work? *Care Knowledge Feature Article 11*: January.

Parton, N. (2104) *The Politics of Child Protection*. London, Palgrave.

Percy-Smith, J. (2005) *What Works in Strategic Partnership Working for Children*. Barkingside: Barnardo's.

Perri 6, Bellamy, C. and Raab, C. (2010) Information-sharing dilemmas in public services: using frameworks from risk management, *Policy and Politics*, 38(3): 465–81.

Perri 6, Leat, D., Seltzer, K. and Stoker, G. (2002) *Towards Holistic Governance, The New Reform Agenda*. Basingstoke: Palgrave.

Perri 6, Raab, C. and Bellamy, C. (2005) Joined-up government and privacy in the United Kingdom: managing tensions between data protection and social policy, Part 1, *Public Administration*, 83(1): 111–33.

Petrioni, P. (1994) Inter-professional teamwork: its history and development in hospitals, general practice and community care (UK), in A. Leathard (ed.) *Going Inter-professional: Working Together for Health and Welfare*. London: Routledge.

Power, M. (1997) *The Audit Society: Rituals of Verification*. Oxford: Oxford University Press.

Puonti, A. (2004) Learning to work together: collaboration between authorities in economic-crime investigation. PhD thesis, University of Helsinki.

Richardson, S. (2007) The challenge of interagency information sharing: a systemic analysis of two Sure Start children's centres. Doctoral thesis, University of Plymouth.

Richardson, S. and Asthana, S. (2005) Policy and legal influences on inter-organisational information sharing in health and social care services, *Journal of Integrated Care*, 13(3): 3–10.

Richardson, S. and Asthana, S. (2006) Inter-agency information sharing in health and social care services: the role of professional culture, *British Journal of Social Work*, 36(4): 657–69.

Robinson, M., Anning, A. and Frost, N. (2005) 'When is a teacher not a teacher?' Knowledge creation and the professional identity of teachers in multi-agency settings, *Studies in Continuing Education*, 27(2): 175–91.

Robinson, M., Atkinson, M. and Downing, D. (2008) *Supporting Theory Building in Integrated Services Research*. Slough: National Foundation for Educational Research.

Rose, J., (2009) *Identifying and Teaching Children and Young People with Dyslexia and Literacy Difficulties*. Nottingham: DCSF Publications.

Rose, W. and Barnes, J. (2008) *Improving Safeguarding Practice: Study of Serious Case Reviews 2001–2003*. London, DCSF.

Rotherham MBC (2014) *The Independent Enquiry into Child Sexual Exploitation in Rotherham 1997–2013*. Accessed 6 June 2015 at: http://www.rotherham.gov.uk/downloads/file/1407/independentinquirycseinrotherham

Salt, T. (2010) *Salt Review: Independent Review of Teacher Supply for Pupils with Severe, Profound and Multiple Learning Difficulties*. Nottingham: DCSF Publications.

Shatzman, L. (1991) Dimensional analysis: notes on an alternative approach to the grounding of theory in qualitative research, in D. Maines (ed.) *Social Organisation and Social Process*. New York: Aldine.

Sheldon Report (1968) *Child Welfare Centres, Public Health*, 82: 52–4.

Sims, D., Fineman, S. and Gabriel, Y. (1993) *Organising and Organisations: An Introduction*. London: Sage.

Skelcher, D., Mathur, N. and Smith, M. (2004) *Effective Partnership and Good Governance: Lessons for Policy and Practice*. Birmingham: INLOGOV.

Sloper, P., Beetham, J., Clarke, S., Franklin, A., Moran, N. and Cusworth, L. (2011) *Transition to Adult Services for Disabled Young People and those with Complex Health Needs. Research Works 2011–02*. York: University of York Social Policy Research Unit.

Solace (2014) *Reclaiming Children's Services*. Policy Report Number Three, April, solace.org.uk

Spivack, R., Craston, M. and Redman, R. (2014) *Evaluation of the SEND Pathfinder Programme Thematic Report: Collaborative working with social care*. London: SQW.

Star, S. and Griesemer, J. (1989) Institutional ecology, 'translations', and boundary objects: amateurs and professionals in Berkeley's Museum of Vertebrate Zoology, 1907–39', *Social Studies of Science*, 19(3): 387–420.

Stewart, J. (1997) The need for community governance, in *A Framework for the Future: An Agenda for Councils in a Changing World*. London: Local Government Information Unit.

Strauss, A. and Corbin, J. (1998) *Basics of Qualitative Research: Techniques and Procedures for Developing Grounded Theory*. London: Sage.

Thom, G., Agbr, M. and Daff, K. (2014) *Evaluation of the SEND Pathfinder Programme Thematic Report: Transition and the engagement of post-16 providers. London: SQW*.

Thornhill, S., Teasedale, G., Murray, G., McEwen, J., Roy, C. and Penny, K. (2000) Disability in young people and adults one year after head injury: prospective cohort study, *British Medical Journal*, 320: 1631–5.

Tushman, M. (1977). 'Special boundary roles in the innovation process', *Administrative Science Quarterly*, 22(4): 587–605.

UNICEF (2007) *Child Poverty in Perspective: An Overview of Child Well Being in Rich Countries*. Florence: UNICEF Innocenti Research Centre.

Wall, K. (2003) *Special Needs and Early Years*. London: Paul Chapman.

Warmington, P., Daniels, H., Edwards, A., Brown, S., Leadbetter, J., Martin, D. and Middleton, D. (2004) *TLRPIII: Learning in and for Interagency Working. Interagency Collaboration: A Review of the Literature*. Birmingham: University of Birmingham.

Warnock, M. (2005) *Special Educational Needs: A New Look. No. 11 in a series of policy discussions*. Salisbury: Philosophy of Education Society of Great Britain.

Wastell, D. and White, S. (2014) Making sense of complex electronic records: socio-technical design in social care, *Applied Ergonomics*, 45: 143–9.

Waters, J., Hatton, C., Crosby, N. and Lazarus, C. (2015) *Report on the Development and Use of POET for Children and Young People with SEND*. Birmingham: In-Control Partnerships.

Watson, D., Townsley, R. and Abbot, D. (2002) Exploring multi-agency working in services to disabled children with complex health care needs and their families, *Journal of Clinical Nursing*, 11(3): 367–75.

Wenger, E. (1998) *Communities of Practice: Learning, Meaning and Identity*. Cambridge: Cambridge University Press.

Whalley, M. and the Pen Green Centre Team (1997) *Involving Parents in their Children's Learning*. London: Paul Chapman.

Wheatley, H. (2006) *Pathways to Success*. London: The Council for Disabled Children.

Yang, T. and Maxwell, T. (2011) Information-sharing in public organizations: a literature review of interpersonal, intra-organizational and inter-organizational success factors, *Government Information Quarterly*, 28 (2): 164–75.

Young, K., Ashby, D., Boaz, A. and Grayson, L. (2002) Social science and the evidence-based policy movement, *Social Policy and Society*, 1(3): 215–24.

Zahir, M. and Bennet, S. (1994) Review of child development teams, *Archives of Disease in Childhood*, 70: 224–8.

Index